# WHAT IF I DON'T HAVE ENOUGH?

## SIMPLE STEPS TO SORT OUT CLUTTER IN YOUR LIFE AND YOUR HOME

RENATA ROBERTS

# CONTENTS

# INTRODUCTION

*In all chaos there is a cosmos, in all disorder a secret order. –Carl Jung*

An essential part of Jung's theory about the concept of chaos illuminates that the *materia confusa* is a crucial element of transformation and that chaos often leads to reorganization. Creating order in the disorder that destroys your enjoyment of life may take some effort, but it is worth every step to get there. We live in overwhelming times and we certainly do not need to feel overwhelmed inside our safe spaces where we revive our souls. External voices are sucking away our lives from our souls, and it can be a frightening experience to listen to the voice of clutter. But we arrive at the first liberating step when we make peace with what our 'stuff' is trying to say to us because the truth is that our 'stuff' says what we, ourselves, cannot say (or simply refuse to say).

Most people are aware of Marie Kondo, who has become a household name when thinking about clutter management. She is famous for saying that things can get messy very quickly in one's environment, and her decluttering advice focuses on keeping only the items that "spark joy" (words made famous through her book

*The Life-Changing Magic of Tidying Up* and Netflix series *Tidying Up With Marie Kondo*) and create a useful and simple response. For this reason, she encourages a mindful approach to organizing our spaces and giving items their rightful spot inside our lives before we decide to let them go.

Apart from this, minimalism has taken a firm foothold in the contemporary world. Marketing teams are making an intentional move toward clean lines and simplicity in their designs, all aiming at enhancing a soothing experience. The #lessisnow and #tiny-house movements are becoming synonymous with the young and trendy new generation who live by a more simplified philosophy of acquiring only quality essentials and living with less for a more sustainable lifestyle, leaving a kinder carbon footprint. The basic concept of both these movements is to create simplicity and serenity, not only physically, but mentally too.

## A DAY IN THE LIFE OF THE 21ST CENTURY

Jenny Jones walks into the living room. She is exhausted after a challenging day at school with colleagues who constantly intrude on her workspace. She feels guilty for yelling at one of them. Her house feels stuffy. Her husband left the TV on and it blares a discordant tone in the background. The dog keeps barking after having spent the whole day waiting for her. She plonks down the file of essays that she still has to mark before tomorrow, and calls a quick 'Hello!' down the hallway with the books and magazines piled up on the floor against the walls. No one answers. Noises and tech sounds emerge behind closed doors from the children's rooms. Her bag drops to the floor with a thud and sprawls out the contents from last month that she never got to rearrange. A half-eaten apple, the aspirin she took for her tension headache last week, random coins, and two perfume bottles all remind her that she has to clean her handbag again. The used tissues have turned solid.

She has to prepare dinner. The kitchen is an absolute mess. The girls made lunch and left their dirty plates and glasses all over the place. Nothing matches. The glasses are chipped from years of use and neglect. They had used the plates that Jenny salvaged from her late mother's home before charity came to distribute the contents. The oven is still on. The kettle is stained from weeks of fingerprints, and the garbage smells of yesterday's fish. The curtains are still drawn. Jenny finds herself thinking, "did I forget to open them this morning, or did I deliberately leave them closed to prevent the neighbors from seeing all our clutter piling up in the kitchen?" She cannot remember.

She tries to find the key to the backdoor, but it's nowhere to be found. She is sure she left it on the kitchen table, but the girls' mobile phones and her husband's gardening tools clutter the space so much that she cannot see anything. She grumbles (but softly) so that she doesn't have to explain her irritation to the others. "How can they not feel ashamed of leaving the house in such a mess? Why do I have to take the burden of it all? I am so tired of trying to organize everything! If only the chaotic thoughts in my head would dissipate a little, I might be able to tackle this physical chaos—but my head is bursting!"

All she wants to do is to sit down in the living room and relax for ten minutes with a glass of white wine before her evening chores, but she cannot. A feeling of dread swamps her and she sighs a heavy breath. The couch is strewn with clothes and ironing that has to be done, boxes of last year's birthday celebrations still lurk on the one side, and the CD collection she wanted to sell is semi-sorted on the other side. It troubles her that she never gets the time to finish the project, but she is completely submerged on all her mental levels. She looks at the *Monstera* in the corner by the window that used to be a lush green, but now droops its thirsty yellowed leaves to the floor. And she feels just like the plant; semi-alive and waiting…

Does this scene sound familiar to you?

"The average person today (1999) receives more information on a daily basis, than the average person received in a lifetime in 1900" (Chrissy, 2021). It is becoming clearer that 'stuff' is replacing our peace of mind. When opening any dictionary, the word "stuff" stirs up clutter with its multitude of definitions. Surely this in itself should be enough reason to consider a more minimalistic approach to how we fill our lives, no? How useful is the 'stuff' that takes up so much space in our lives? How much 'stuff' do we 'stuff' our souls with, until we feel as overburdened as Mrs. Jones?

Some typical pain points of our times have been highlighted in recent years. Artificial intelligence and the technological revolution, climate change and the energy crisis, pollution, a sharp rise in global famine and inequality, terrorism, the COVID-19 pandemic, increasing rates of depression, and now a threatening potential-world war in Ukraine swamp our lives. Some of the biggest issues in the world are combating poverty, hunger, religious war, food and water supplies in remote and underprivileged areas, as well as health problems in developing nations. The youth are particularly exposed to a mental health crisis with far-reaching consequences. They feel hopeless, and many youngsters are living with a fear of missing out (FOMO), excessive drug abuse exposure, coping with eating disorders, self-harming tendencies, and general fear for their future on our planet. The post-pandemic global tendency to experience a fear of lack and FOMO has also reared its head.

Not every problem is a mess and not every mess is a problem. But the stigma of clutter and the demands of a contemporary lifestyle—involving keeping in line with the Joneses, social bombardment, information overload, and so on—make us feel overwhelmed at some point. The Joneses used to be the next-door neighbors, but now they have evolved into celebrities who assail us on social media platforms and from e-commerce driven by corporate profit. Consumerism dictates our lifestyles and advertising firms specifically focus on our perceived needs via television, radio, smart devices, GPS, and anything digital that can clutter our hands and homes. They are relentlessly bombarding us with their deficit advertising by saying that we are not enough and do not have enough. We respond with a misplaced sense of belonging somewhere, or by accumulating more stuff, only to end up with not only cluttered homes, but cluttered minds as well. Eventually, we have to rent more space to accommodate the extra stuff that we cannot keep with us, but are reluctant to let go of. And it all gathers dust while our minds clutter even more because we are constantly chasing time to manage it all.

How psychological is clutter? Well, think of it this way: Our stuff is a mirror. It mirrors our fears and hopes, and the way that our minds work. Is it that you don't have enough, or that you just have too much? Many people forget that they already have the things they think they really need, and then end up with stuff that gets in the way. Psychologists believe a subconscious drive feeds the process of accumulating and multidimensional hoarding. The words "I can't" are becoming paralyzing mind clutter for many individuals, preventing them from experiencing a joyful life.

Many people overspend their budgets in the process of senseless accumulation. Waste spending has a global cluttering effect. We just have to look at the cost of recycling fast fashion and poorly made items that end up hoarding the African continent after First World countries throw them away. Clutter costs us our time, money, and focus. Did you really have to buy that sale item that you never wear? Or the shoes you bought in a hurry while feeling overwhelmed after a stressful day at work?

The idea is not to make you feel more burdened by reading this. In fact, be assured that you are not alone, nor broken, nor a lost cause. You are simply part of modern society, which is exposing you to its overwhelming pressures. A messy life is shared by many others. Below are some stats that prove you are not unique in this regard. I hope these will create some encouragement for making a change!

- 91% of survey respondents confirmed they would be happier if they had more order in their lives.
- We spend one year of our lives looking for lost things (stop and think about that.)
- More than four hours per week are spent searching for digital documents.
- 40% of housework can be eliminated by reducing the clutter in our homes.
- 23% of adults admit that they lose bills and then forget to pay them, with resultant penalties.
- 80% of items that we choose to keep are never used.
- A study in 2019 found that the average American spent around $18,000 per year on non-essential goods.
- British researchers found that the average ten-year-old child only plays with 12 of their 238 toys.
- 32% of women have a whopping number of more than 25 pairs of shoes in their wardrobes.
- 78% of people have no idea what to do with all their clutter...
- Statistics about the amounts of storage renting are even more upsetting!
- And statistic lists are longer than your average grocery list...

Statistics overlap globally, while some fluctuate in various cultures and over continents. Regularly updated data only proves our useless chasing after stuff, as consumers in a global and market-orientated world keep accumulating more. Post-pandemic data also shows significant changes. After being forced to spend so much time at home, we became more aware of the influence of our surroundings. All the time spent at home inspired us to be creative and more aware of organizing, upcycling, and repurposing. Most of us have become more tech knowledgeable as well, since we had to do almost everything online, adding to all of our mental overloads.

Many people have the same issues and fears about clutter as you do. Many have taken on the challenge of decluttering, and successfully found some relief and joy in a simpler life. Simply removing one thing (that does not add value) from your life daily and maintaining the process, definitely contributes to a sense of tranquility and order in the chaos. So, what is the solution? The main idea is to focus on how our lives can be more meaningful and better with less stuff, physically, digitally, and mentally. Do we really have to keep all of our dear departed Grandma's doilies? First, we have to ask the question of letting go or not. If we make a committed choice of a more healthy and simplified lifestyle, then we have to focus on the value and purpose of an item before we keep it or discard it. The final step is to maintain the habit, while keeping our goals in mind. In this way, we release gratitude and find freedom, unencumbered by external trappings.

So, why is cluttering such a big problem for people? Let's find out. Making peace with our stuff, is making peace with ourselves.

# 1

# FROM CLUTTER TO CLARITY

Do you want to change, or do you need to change? There is a difference between can't and won't. Jung said in his lectures, "The old idea of chaos was that it held everything in potential, even man" (Purrington, 2020). Clutter keeps us fluttering, while clarity creates calm. So, how do we break through the barrier of clutter to reach tranquility?

## THE STIGMA OF CLUTTER

Psychologists interpret a multitude of meanings from our surrounding clutter. They even say that a too clean house may reveal things about someone's character. In that case, what does our clutter say about us? Are the number of things that we buy and display in our homes a revelation of our state of mind? We may be surprised to learn the truth. Noah Mankowski, a clinical psychologist who specializes in hoarding syndrome, says that "The way you perceive your clutter is the way you perceive yourself and your relationships" (Hone, 2017). He adds that our placement of clutter in a home may even relate to the different emotions from related events. Clutter in our living areas may indicate issues in our social lives, while in the bathroom it may represent body issues, and so forth.

A more contemporary branch of psychology emphasizes an alternative approach of positive reinforcement focusing on character strengths and behavior. The aim is to assist with building more meaningful and purposeful lives. Positive psychology promotes living a more enjoyable and flourishing life, instead of merely surviving. The movement has proved to be beneficial in improving deep, meaningful satisfaction and well-being, as opposed to fleeting happiness. The term "flow state" is associated with this movement, implying full immersion and enjoyment during the process of the activity, ultimately resulting in energized focus and mindful involvement. It additionally encourages character strengths and virtues, proving its point of difference from other psychological branches. The difference is due to the primary focus on building and identifying assets instead of focusing on mental problems and weaknesses. Although it is a fairly recent contribution to the field since its introduction in the late 1990s, many of its concepts are based on humanistic psychology (Abraham Maslow also coined the term "positive psychology") from the 1950s.

So, how do we apply positive psychology to decluttering our lives in general? If we focus on courage, humanity, and gratitude, then we already apply positivity. It simply means removing one item to set the motion on due course. It does not, however, imply that negative perceptions should be ignored, and positive psychologists advise reflection time on these mood states. It is believed that people who flourish in meaningful environments have the capacity to overcome these momentary lapses. Researchers have found that people who find their lives worthwhile generally have improved mental and physical health when well-being is coupled with having a sense of purpose.

When we clutter areas so that we cannot see things, we believe we don't have to deal with them. At some point in our lives, we were all told by parents or significant others to clean up our rooms. The paradigm remained stuck. Being messy and disorganized became stigmatized, and the experience of disorder remained ingrained in our minds. Did you become an organized hoarder because of this? There is a fine line between healthy and unhealthy clutter... The question is *can* you or *won't* you make changes?

### *Hoarder Disorder*

Hoarding behavior should not be compared to obsessive-compulsive (OCD) behavior. It may be related to OCD, but hoarder disorder does not always exhibit OCD symptoms. In 2016, Janet Spittlehouse found in her research study about hoarding behaviors and related well-being, that "High harm avoidance and low self-directedness were strongly associated with poorer self-reported mental and physical health and increased hoarding behaviours. Hoarding disorder was strongly associated with economic hardship and impairment of mental and physical functioning."

The debilitating psychopathological behavior of hoarding was only officially recognized independently of other compulsive disorders in the Diagnostic and Statistical Manual of Mental Disorders (DSM-5) in 2013. Hoarding disorder is defined as the continuous difficulty of throwing things away, regardless of their specific value. This is accompanied by increased distress and impairment resulting from hoarding behavior, unusefulness of particular living areas due to the clutter, and distress resulting from having to save items for no particular reason. It is thus clear that hoarding interferes with a person's healthy functioning, which makes it very different from being purely disorganized or messy. Compulsive hoarding eventually interferes with a person's relationships, career, and family life. A messy or disorganized person will at some point remove the stuff that gets in the way, while a hoarder will have psychological difficulty with this.

Apart from the low levels of self-control that may cause and maintain hoarding behavior, other variables for high hoarding scores involve trauma, unemployment, socio-economic status, being single, and lower-income levels. The comorbidity of depression shows an additional 50% link to hoarding disorder, and the prevalence of anxiety also contributes to hoarding. Impulsivity levels increase with compulsive hoarding according to various studies. The core issue of hoarder identity is the wounding of the soul. The items possess the hoarder and not the other way round. Material things become their source of happiness, and letting go is almost impossible because the clutter provides safety and comfort.

Hoarders often feel embarrassed and ashamed when other people see the mess. They do not display their items like collectors, even though they are actually accumulating tangible items. Simply cleaning up the area does not solve the underlying issue and often leaves the hoarder feeling more lost, especially if they did not authorize the process. The chances of relapse are high unless the psychological issues are addressed and acknowledged holistically, with sincere support. A holistic approach to the complexities of hoarding seems to be the only successful recovery system. Because hoarding is a multifaceted issue, it requires assistance from a team of professionals for support, and thus a long-term treatment plan is more effective.

Stereotyping people with hoarder stigma may just increase the distress. Most of them have an impaired ability to make decisions; they are not simply lazy or dirty. Hoarding may also be a major result of not being able to cope with grief after a major loss. It is therefore important to know that compassion and empathy are necessary for the healing process, while judgment and being overly critical will not help.

### *PTSD*

Trauma has a paralyzing effect on the person. Unexpected trauma has the ability to overwhelm. Trauma and hoarding are, furthermore, closely linked. It has been found that most hoarders who also show signs of OCD suffered from at least one traumatic incident during their lives. The general explanation is that people try to fill a void from experiencing loss by replacing the emotion with tangible items. Many individuals with PTSD get overly excited about acquiring these items and they will give detailed explanations and justifications for the conditions of finding them. Removing these items from their homes creates tremendous stress. Researchers have confirmed that compulsive shopping is a common coping mechanism for dealing with grief and post-traumatic stress.

After a traumatic event, stress levels rise while creating new links in the brain that spark a reaction to fear. This produces higher cortisol levels, which remain in limbo and are fed by further stress. A cycle ensues where the mind is cluttered with fear from the trauma. PTSD furthermore affects different areas of the brain, but the frontal parts (which are the self-care areas directly related to disorganization) are affected the most, which is why so many individuals end up feeling distressed from their resulting chaotic environments and mental clutter.

Circumstances in which we have to cope with the loss of a family member and sort out their estate, can be a highly challenging process that amasses emotional clutter on top of the trauma. Many individuals take a long time to work through the process, and some people simply postpone or ignore the activity. This is because dramatic changes are extremely challenging and often create a feeling of being stuck. It is often in these circumstances that the 'dread pile' starts to increase and gather dust. This is normal because the individual is left exhausted with overwhelming emotions, as well as most of the time, with simply too much to do. Patience in these circumstances is crucial. Useful advice from professionals is to prioritize, make a date to do something, make the event pleasant by listening to your favorite music, reward yourself, and ask for support from trusted friends. These times are also useful to reflect on where the clutter generally appears in your life. Facing and processing this creates mindful awareness of your habits.

### *Anxiety*

Most of us experience some kind of worry, stress, or anxiety on a daily basis. The difference is when it interferes with our healthy functioning and coping. There is a difference between the three. Worry is basically focused on negative outcomes, such as things that could go wrong. The mind dwells on these things, while they stay only in the mind. The body does not show a response to worry. Worrying about something can actually have a positive effect on calming the brain during a tense situation, for example an exam. Still, worry is only beneficial if it enables change, not when it turns into obsessive overthinking that does not contribute to any positive outcomes.

Stress is the normal physiological response to an external trigger, so it is basically a reaction to changes in the environment, which in turn depletes our coping resources. Imagine coming across a bear on your Sunday afternoon stroll—this creates stress! The limbic system responds with the production of increased adrenaline and cortisol that activate a response, usually in the form of a rapid heart rate, sweaty palms, heavy breathing, and so forth. But, there is a big difference between acute stress and chronic stress. The former is a short-term response to obtain a goal, while the latter keeps the body in a fight-or-flight mode that doesn't resolve itself because the stressor remains (e.g. financial strain, a narcissistic boss), which keeps causing digestive problems, heart issues, and deteriorating immune system problems. The best way to combat stress is with regular exercise, effective time management, and maintaining control of the stressors and your response to them.

Anxiety is more difficult to control. It is the persistent combination of stress and worries, meaning that it is experienced in the mind, as well as in the body. The difference here is that with stress there is a threat, but with anxiety, there is none, or often only a false alarm or misinterpretation leading to the emotion. A good example can be an early morning encounter with a boss who looks angry and whom you assume is upset with you, or that you may lose your job (even though he did not say or do anything to support this assumption). Your body experiences the same symptoms, but there is no visible bear on the path! Sometimes anxiety is based on fears, and in many cases, it is rooted in childhood abuse or past traumatic experiences that were not resolved. In severe cases, anxiety disorders (substance-induced anxiety disorder, separation anxiety disorder, agoraphobia, generalized anxiety disorder, social anxiety disorder or phobia, and specific phobias) develop that require professional guidance. They are serious medical conditions that can interfere with a person's normal functioning, and in some cases, they may be life-threatening.

Thinking your way out of anxiety is not always possible, and sometimes anxiety can trigger panic attacks. Risk factors for anxiety disorders include personality type, medical stressors, drug and alcohol-related factors, trauma, and stress build-up. Apart from the physical effects on the body, anxiety may contribute to depression and feelings of worthlessness, social isolation, poor life quality, and may also generally interfere with daily functioning.

The key is how to use worry, stress, and anxiety in a positive way to enable change in our lives, along with helping us with the decluttering process.

## WHAT IS YOUR CLUTTER IDENTITY?

The root beliefs around having a messy life revolve around our identities. As children and adolescents, we were influenced by events and significant others that formed conditioning patterns, and as adults, we unconsciously apply them to every aspect of our lives. The world is filled with unique human beings who have their own journeys and conditioned stories to share, and none are the same. This shows in our clutter. Our clutter has unique identities and stories, just like us. Identifying our personal clutter identity makes it easier to tackle decluttering with a lighthearted approach toward a more harmonious space.

Our clutter habits create some relatable archetypes, including:

- The procrastinator always has something else that takes priority.
- Justincaser preaches that you never know—you may just fit into that size of jeans again, so it's best to keep them.
- Dragon loves to hoard as much as possible so that he becomes invisible.
- Fun-focused cannot be bothered about aesthetic appearances in the home since he's living the life and has no time for frivolities.
- Painful Penny is holding on to the past—and counting the losses with every fridge magnet that reminds her of better days in better places, or worse—the places she regrets never visiting.
- Sentimental cannot let those memories go—she stores the loss of every moment in an item on her bookshelf.

- Sunk Cost Fallacy proves frugality pays because he paid so much for an item even though he never uses it, that the financial value keeps it out of the garbage bin.
- Beauty Queen simply has a love affair with her beauty products and she cannot let the last drop go. It will eventually get out of the tub if she has time one day to force it out. Is she holding on to a fading youth or trying to perfect something that society forces upon her?
- Resourceful has to simply keep all the paperwork and invoice slips because he never knows when the computer may crash and let him lose them all. The paper nemesis follows him everywhere.
- Miss Stylish loves clothes too much and doesn't stop adding more. Well, it's time to donate that dress with the price tag hanging in the back of the wardrobe. Someone else may just be more grateful for its use and even use it more than once.
- Good Mother has to save all the Legos that she used to curse about when she stepped on them on the way to her crying child's room in the middle of the night.
- Crafty Cat always needs a new unfinished project, as the others pile up while she enjoys her siesta on the sofa. She avoids the rule of not buying any unfinished projects (like the three-legged chair) that will clutter her home and never be fixed anyway. She knows it is more meaningful to spend time with the kids on the beach. She will book a project day next month and invite friends over to join the fixing activity, but not today...

Clutter closely aligns with our shadow side—the thing that we fear the most is what ironically happens to us and it often shows up from our clutter. We overcompensate for our fear by becoming a clutter archetype with a specific identity. The solution is understanding the cause. The idea is to create balance and strike a harmonious chord that supports our specific environment.

## YOUR NEEDS, WANTS, AND DESIRES

It is important to identify your personal reason for wanting to declutter. What are your most important needs? What do you want to achieve? Do you desire something specific? Do you feel out of control? Most people have a predetermined idea of what is important to them. Sometimes, though, life takes over and we lose track of these while we keep hovering in the marsh of our reality. Clutter swamps our lives and we give up trying to maintain harmony, only to find our mental conditions deteriorating and our relationships suffering as a result.

## HOW BAD IS IT REALLY?

When researching hoarder syndrome, psychotherapist Renee M. Winters became aware of the intimate connection between people and their clutter. She discovered that clutter could be blamed for keeping hoarders deliberately separated from intimate connections with family members, companions, friends, and life itself. She tried to determine during her sessions with famous hoarder personalities (like Andy Warhol) whether the hoarding and separation were done unknowingly, if the reason behind it was driven by fear of emotional chaos or control issues, or if the syndrome involved issues with deeper human connection issues with themselves and with others. She explains the hoarding issue as "a crisis of the soul" (Winters, 2016), which elevates intense mental stress underlying the actual hoarding and cluttering.

Your stress and anxiety levels are the best indicators of change. The clutter may be speaking to you through your physical symptoms resulting from stress and anxiety. Perhaps you experience a daily panic attack when you enter your kitchen, just like Jenny Jones? Maybe your palms are sweaty when you open your wardrobe and look at all those shoes? Perhaps the stigma is still stuck from your mother's constant screaming at you for not tidying up your room? Do the clutter archetypes sound familiar to you? All these symptoms are real indications that change is needed. From clutter to clarity, it takes only the first step. The rest will follow!

2

# THE CONSEQUENCES OF CHAOS

If we understand the reciprocal effect that clutter has on us, we may find more motivation to make a change. Clutter is not so much about casting away or letting go, but about gaining something more valuable: time, harmony, space, energy, and freedom.

## THE MESS EFFECT

How does the brain react to mental and physical clutter? Researchers have found that clutter affects our brains cumulatively because the constant reminders of disorganization drain our cognitive resources and overload our brains. Our brains prefer order, and the continuous visual reminders of disorder reduce our focus and working memory. They are furthermore becoming aware of the relationship between clutter and stress levels. Clutter significantly increases cortisol (a stress hormone) levels in the brain. The general feeling is that when you have to move things around in your environment in order to do something, you already have a stress-inducing clutter problem. They also discovered that clutter is generally linked with procrastination. None of us enjoy clearing our mailboxes from all the daily junk mail and marketing. As a result, the mess simply intensifies, and the cycle of frustration and anxiety is fed by neglect and senseless hoarding.

Assistant psychology professor Darby Saxbe from the University of Southern California found that women who perceived their homes as cluttered generally start their day in a stressed state and remain stressed during the rest of the day, especially with the added housework and chores that they tend to take on after work. Dr. Saxbe found that "Clutter is in the eye of the beholder" and that "The people who talked about it were the ones who had the cortisol response" (Le Beau Lucchesi, 2019). This is merely one research study that highlights the negative correlation between clutter and stress. The mess effect is real. Regaining control over decluttering drudgery becomes a never-ending challenge. And the physical clutter outside contributes to the mental clutter inside.

## AS WITHOUT, SO WITHIN

Raised cortisol levels leading to higher anxiety is merely one example of the negative correlation of clutter and our well-being. Low fight-or-flight levels that persist subconsciously and exhaust our survival resources, struggling with illnesses or digestion maintenance, and even weight issues all contribute to the deterioration of our health. It has been found that participants from organized and minimalistic homes show higher productivity, better health, and generally higher activity levels.

Apart from having effects on our bodies and daily functioning; increased blood pressure, digestion problems, interference with sleep patterns, and unhealthy dust collecting clutter causing respiratory issues—all contribute to physical deterioration. Clutter can become a fire hazard and it has been found that it negatively impacts people's eating habits as well. It simply becomes too much effort to prepare food, and so people revert to takeout and fast food preparation that ultimately impact their eating habits and health, and ultimately breeds more clutter. But what does clutter do to our internal perceptions?

### *Visual and Mental Distractions*

Clutter has the nasty tendency to clutter our minds and destroy our mental capacity. The negative feelings make us dwell and over-think about the 'stuff' until we eventually think negatively about ourselves as well. Our overwhelming clutter has the ability to cause "decision fatigue"—in other words, excess clutter makes us hesitant to start something or make choices. It further enhances memory loss, because the chaos inside our exhausted brains forgets important information that we have to remember. Clutter also distracts us from focusing on the things that really matter, like spending time with people instead of spending our time organizing the chaos. It keeps stealing our focus and distracting us until nothing gets done.

### *Overstimulation*

Visual overload leads to the inability to process visually and accurately. It has been found that random stimuli cluttering an environment make it harder to read people's feelings. Facial expressions and body language are being overpowered by visual stimuli that distract us. Too much stuff also steals our tranquility because of its burdening effect, since it earns more to maintain it, and the related effort to keep up the maintenance leaves us exhausted. Overstimulation eventually reduces our productivity levels.

### *Overwhelm*

Too much clutter makes us feel like we are losing control. We perceive the day as being too short to care for all the stuff that needs our attention. Feeling constantly inadequate or out of control leads to poor self-control. It makes us feel discouraged from allowing ourselves to bring things into our home over time without true intention. It is much more difficult to reverse the feeling of being overwhelmed than to prevent it with mindful attention to value before we add another responsibility to our lives. Eventually, we end up feeling hopeless and negative about ourselves, as well as our homes. Hopelessness is further fed by the overwhelming emotion of not being able to change our habits or do anything about the accumulating clutter. This feeds the accumulation cycle, as we try to numb out or avoid the emotions by buying more. In severe cases, the feeling of hopelessness may also lead to dangerous self-destructive behaviors. Too many objects and feelings of overwhelm lead to the false resolution of acquiring more space to accommodate everything. But what we actually need is to get rid of some stuff, because more space simply allows for more clutter, if we do not address the root issue.

### *Lost Items*

The terrible cycle of not finding our things in a cluttered space, then purchasing more to replace those lost items, only to find the original item later, is something we have all experienced. The simple solution is to have less and to organize things better, so that every item has its place. If every household member maintains the order and puts items back in their place immediately after use, the problem gets resolved without ever having to look for something. The problem that arises, though, is that this concept is not so easy to maintain. Life has become overly complicated, and while it's normal to lose things on a daily basis, a cluttered life piles on additional pressure, making us lose focus.

### *Wasted Time*

Our excess stuff literally steals our time from us! Every object does not only take up space, but also our time and effort. Think about it this way:

Everything you own takes some of your time. First, you need to work to earn the money to buy it. Then shop for it, pick it up, organize it, put it away, repair it, maintain it, look for it, etc. Even if it doesn't seem like much time, when you multiply those few seconds multiple times a day by every single item you own, it adds up. It can often feel like you have a never-ending to-do list just taking care of all your stuff! (Simple Lionheart Life, 2019)

When items hold high value for us, they justify the time spent on them because they return something. That being said, we have to constantly reassess if we truly only keep the things that do not steal our time, otherwise, we end up wasting time on less important matters.

### *Anxiety*

Clutter affects our moods negatively. Constantly having to look at all the things that are in the way requires attention from us, and this tends to make us feel depressed. This, in turn, makes it harder to destress. The frustration leads to irritability that affects everybody around us. Our increased stress levels are constantly bombarded with the number of things to be dealt with as a matter of urgency. This has a negative effect on our relationships, behavior, and physical health by causing higher blood pressure, increased heart rate, and breathing difficulties. It has been found that clutter even controls our eating habits, and depending on individual anxiety coping mechanisms, individuals may either overeat or undereat. Essentially, we sacrifice our peace and quality of life for a few extra objects that do not contribute in value to our enjoyment, nor to our sense of peace inside our homes.

### *Being Less Productive*

Too much attention to our clutter reduces our mental and physical energy levels. We spend more time cleaning the clutter, organizing the clutter, and even thinking about organizing or removing the clutter all the time. It becomes an exhausting process of worrying about stuff that does not need our concerns! We end up feeling that we are spinning wheels without ever getting ahead. This lack of focus on what is really important also makes us lose our intention to create balance in our lives.

### *Coping and Avoidance Strategies*

We feel hopeless and accumulate negative feelings when we see how much has to be done. This often leads to procrastination when we feel overwhelmed by the daunting task of starting to clear the clutter everywhere. Our homes should be sanctuaries that we can enjoy with our families, but instead, we try to avoid the cluttered space called home. We maintain a lifestyle of merely coping with the mess, procrastinating the urgency to organize it all, and avoiding reality. Hoarders often feel embarrassed about having people in their homes. They avoid social interaction altogether or excessively apologize for the appearance of their homes. Both lead to higher levels of anxiety, increased distress, and lower levels of self-worth.

### *Relationships*

Clutter has the nasty habit of confusing our priorities. We end up spending more time managing the clutter instead of spending time with the people who matter in our lives. Clutter is distracting and diverts our attention away from people and, ultimately, our relationships suffer because of this. We get annoyed at having to spend too much time organizing and rearranging the clutter and then take it out on family members. Or, in severe cases, we avoid socializing as a result of bad time management.

### *Wealth and Health*

When we think of objects in monetary terms, we tend to change our perception of their value and necessity. Everything we own was once money in our hands... Objects bought impulsively or with emotional intent often end up becoming clutter that does not bring lasting joy. These objects also stretch our budgets because we buy them without planning. If we consider the value of money in our bank accounts in comparison to the extra stuff in our homes, I think the former wins. Clutter has the ability to destroy our contentment. Too much clutter interferes with our sense of pleasure in our homes, making us feel more stressed inside the space that's meant to be a sanctuary. People relate strongly to their living environment, and therefore a cluttered environment negatively impacts moods, making us feel more 'cranky.'

## THE EFFECT OF TOO MUCH COMPLEXITY

Most psychoses result from too much life complexity. We break at our weakest point. If we keep this in mind and make a mental change in perception of what clutter really is and the consequences of the chaos, we discover an awareness that propels us into action.

Clutter should not be seen as things to lose, but rather as things to simplify into harmony. Material, technological, psychological, relational, and societal complexity demand too much from us on a daily basis. The solution is simplifying and organizing complexities in order to gain something more useful. What we gain must have a higher value, like freedom and tranquility. The goal is simplicity—not simply to lose stuff.

Sometimes, our mess may just be a result of bad habits: We come home and toss the keys on the table, kick off our shoes on the kitchen floor, and leave the TV remote on the couch, because it is too much effort to be organized. Clutter persists and breeds itself in this way if we do not deliberately organize against these habits. A shoe rack at the door, a TV remote basket by the screen, a key hook in the hallway, and the deliberate habit of placing these things where they belong will bring you a sensation of harmony. Clutter does not necessarily mean that we have too many things, it may simply be a matter of not organizing them well. Simplifying and organizing has the effect of balancing our mental state.

Our homes should be retreats, not prisons. Our minds should be calm, not anxious.

# 3

# BEHIND THE MESS

For many people, the concept of "if worshiping" becomes a competition between what they truly need and what really happens in their lives. The words "If I surround myself with more things, I will feel less alone" may be a constant "if" statement in your life that makes you overspend in order to accumulate more things. You end up spending copious amounts of time behind screens to accumulate things and ideas that other people tell you that you need. Have you asked yourself why? You simply end up with rooms stuffed with stuff and a mind stuffed with strings of thought. This disorganization is not the real problem; we need to get to the root of the issue.

## FEAR, STRESS, AND TRAUMA

These are the most common fears behind the mess. Addressing them reduces and maintains clutter habits. We have all encountered trauma in some form during our lives. We all face unavoidable stressful situations, and we all have conditioned fears that disrupt our enjoyment of life. Perhaps it's time to address them?

*Fear of Lack*

Many of us waste our lives living with the fear of "not having" —not having the money to do things, the time to read all the books we want to read, the energy to organize our house, the patience to sort out toxic relationships, or simply not having the wisdom to get through one overwhelming day. Yet, even though everything is always seen in the worst-case scenario, we still end up 'having' in abundance. This is called the fear of "not enough," and it drives our consumerist approach to cram more into our already overfilled lives. We end up feeling frenzied, trying to fix everything, and unable to enjoy what we do have, all while we focus only on the lack of things we don't have. We constantly compete and compare ourselves and our lives to others in order to compensate for this lack. And all this does is drain our resources and chase up our anxiety levels. A scarcity mindset is basically "A persistent feeling of not-enoughness–feelings of inadequacy, fear of going without, a lack of self-confidence–most often stemming from negative thought patterns around time, money and energy" (Fallon, 2015). This mindset is not based on our bank balance, but rather on our feelings of self-worth and how we perceive ourselves in relation to others.

This is where the media and 21st-century social and digital bombardment come in. Our beliefs are based on our interpretation of past experiences. So, if we were conditioned by significant others or events that often made us feel diminished in the past, we are driven to overcompensate the feeling in some way in the present. The media knows this, and advertising companies are bombarding us thousands of times each day with material replacements for this feeling of inferiority or lack. We end up subconsciously fighting this fear of lack while society thrives on our misinterpretation of emotions. This leaves us feeling frantic, overworked, and frequently confused.

Some people hoard things to prevent a future disaster, often ironically cluttering their homes to a state of unlivability in the present moment. We have all lived through a recent pandemic, with periods of lockdowns resulting in restrictive access to anything that is not deemed 'essential.' How many of us hoarded the toilet paper before the impending doom, only to find that we survived anyway? I remember from years of living in a remotely semi-arid area in Africa how material things acquired a new value. Running out of supplies when your nearest dealer is a bumpy two-hour drive away on dirt roads makes you plan your life better. What I have also learned from that period is that human beings are very innovative and we can adapt to survive. Being mindful of value makes us more resilient and more accepting of impending disasters because we know we have the ability to outlive them, and we do not focus on what we do not have. So, the vicious cycle of fear of lack can only be broken when we focus on the moment and priorities. Laughing about the lack of toilet paper with your family is much more meaningful than wasting all that energy on the fear that you might run out while the children fall over the stacked paper.

Have an abundance mindset. Simply change the story that you tell yourself about your fear of lack by assuring yourself that there is enough. Tell yourself that not only is your world enough, but that you are enough inside your world. Be open to receiving that abundance, even if it occasionally comes with challenges and some momentary lack—because your enjoyment of life depends on more. Be attentive to the flow movement in and out of your life and enjoy it. Release what you do not need, value your blessings, and never feel compelled to give more than you have.

### *Fear of Loss and Change*

Fear of loss and change are both related to individual attachment styles that were conditioned in childhood. Grief is a natural consequence of loss and it takes on different forms depending on the loss itself. Loss from death, where motives are not questioned except in the case of suicide, exhibits different grief symptoms than a break-up with a significant person. Attachment styles (thinking patterns, behaviors, and feelings that maintain our connections) are activated during times of loss and change as coping mechanisms for grief and to regain security. These styles are established in childhood depending on parental conditioning and environmental influences. Insecure attachment styles often procure less post-traumatic growth and more grief.

Four distinct types are:

- Secure attachment – with consistently responsive and available parents, a child learns to perceive and respond accurately to other people because their security does not feel threatened. They learn to manage their emotions in a healthy way.
- Avoidant attachment – rejecting a child's desire for closeness and withholding reassurance damages the child's security and presents dismissive connections in adulthood. The individual denies their emotions and need for close relationships.
- Anxious attachment – inconsistent parental styles condition children to constantly monitor the parents' moods for their own security to avoid rejection. In adulthood, they are preoccupied and always on guard to avoid abandonment signals. These individuals find change, grieving, and loss challenging because they try to remain as close as possible to loved ones. They also struggle to rationalize and understand loss and change.
- Disorganized attachment – these parental environments are highly volatile, unpredictable, and

> insecure (mostly related to violence, victimization, being terrorized, bullying, or frightening situations), which lead to unresolved and disorganized attachment styles in adult life. The parents can be frightened themselves or project their frightening emotions onto the child. Because they never learn how to cope with loss, these individuals find it extremely hard to deal with loss into adulthood, mostly resulting from their former unresolved traumas that led to PTSD.

Attachment styles influence the way a person grieves. Furthermore, there are different ways to grieve after loss and it is not always an indication of the intensity of love for the deceased or lost person. Someone can be heartbroken over a not-so-close connection, but then show little emotive response to an intimate and much-loved connection. Some grieve for years after the loss and sometimes hold on to the loss merely to avoid losing a sense of caring for the deceased person.

When our security feels threatened by either loss or change, we respond with our defense and coping mechanisms. Any positive life changes are often inhibited by our fear of the unknown. Change can be frightening and demand new unfamiliar and challenging behaviors. Fear of change also implicates fear of surprises. Human beings attach to their comfort zones and feel secure with familiarity. An effective strategy to cope with change is to investigate the consequences of the act.

Change can be hampered by spontaneity and this is why structure and routine are important aspects to maintain simplicity. Categorize items (or cluttered thoughts) into valuable, neutral, or not useful, and then organize them and eliminate the ones that are not useful. Review and re-evaluate your plan daily to assist with change and remember that repetition enhances the probability of success. When things have a logical sequence and order, they declutter our minds as well as our rooms.

### *Fear of Judgment and Rejection*

Gabor Maté explains the concept of abandonment as an inseparable combination of biology and emotions. What we lose emotionally translates to a biological response in the body. In his YouTube video, *How Your Past Trauma Really Works* (Maté, 2022), we learn how past trauma, emotions, and rejection create a stressful state that persists into adult life. When a child feels abandoned and can't escape or when the fight-or-flight response is triggered but neither fight or flight is possible, dissociation becomes a coping response to enduring the feelings of helplessness. If this remains constant, it eventually becomes a social pathology. What is meant to be a temporary coping mechanism becomes a long-term dysfunctional habit in adulthood. The trauma of abandonment forced the brain to develop in a certain way in relation to its specific environment. The necessary conditions for optimal brain development are emotionally non-stressed, non-depressed, and consistently available parents who remain attuned to the child. Any interference that doesn't offer this to the child affects brain development and it remains an emotionally implicit memory of the fear of rejection that shows in adult responses.

It is believed that rejection in childhood is one of the most complex traumatic experiences to deal with in adult life and it requires consistent and professional intervention to eliminate and manage the fear. Most healing practices focus on understanding, acknowledgment, and mindfulness as a holistic solution to recovery. It has also been found that babies respond closely and negatively to their mother's fears and stress. The brain eventually develops an adaptation to tuning out as a response to cope with the stress and lack of an emotionally present mother. It has further been found that if the emotional needs of a child are not met, it creates a conducive space for the development of personality disorders.

One of the most powerful fears related to rejection is the fear of being judged. It prevents you from expressing yourself and keeps you trapped in a non-authentic life. The fear is simply your ego telling you that your safety is threatened based on a past childhood fear of being abandoned (for a child, rejection feels like a death sentence). In adult life, the fear remains as a feeling of losing something or alienation. We are not born with this fear, but it develops as part of societal norms to avoid ridicule. Social media is the worst medium for judgment in our times, and the more we expose ourselves to the platform, the more we increase our judgment ratios.

The fear of judgment is a daily necessity that keeps us safe, but it becomes a prison when we do not process the fear and allow it to sabotage us. Teenagers live with intense emotions of fear of judgment, and if the tools to manage these external opinions are not offered to them, the words remain stuck, affect their self-esteem, and hamper their lives continuously. To manage the ratio of judgment in our lives, we have to be aware that the more people who are listening or paying attention to us, the higher the number of those who can judge us. We also have to force ourselves to be mindful of the fact that if we always live by others' compliments, then their criticisms will surely destroy us. It is, therefore, crucial to remind ourselves that one person's opinion does not equal the whole world's perspective. We harness positive feelings from being seen, heard, and valued. This is positive judging that humans have to feel at their core being.

Three prominent techniques to implement change are, first, to speak your truth (especially about the things you feel passionate about), because this makes the need to be heard by others bigger than the fear of their judgment. Secondly, surround yourself with people who enhance and support you, but guard against prioritizing one person's opinion over yours. Thirdly, and still the best solution, is to accept and almost welcome judgment—you always have a choice. If you choose to respect a comment (after mindful reflection) or to hate it, you give yourself the ability and the power to reframe it quickly. This enhances your understanding that the perspective of the commenter stands separately from yours. It creates a defense against judgments that are bound to come your way and fosters an environment where you do not constantly feel that you have to hide and protect yourself from the 'harsh' world.

### *FOMO*

"Fear of missing out" (FOMO) has become a household term in modern life. It is based on the fear of us missing out on the things in life that we desire. We perceive losing things in various scenarios; it can be financial profit, a social life, or material things, and the extreme dissatisfaction of missing out may lead to intense frustration and sadness. FOMO is often associated with loneliness, anxiety, and depression and is caused by fear. The question we have to ask ourselves is whether the fear is driven by having missed out in general or not having the things we miss. It may be a frightening idea of purely missing that 'something,' or being the odd one out, and even being judged for not being somewhere.

This brings us to the root of the issue, the element of comparison that constitutes FOMO: Are we experiencing a fear of loss or of seeing the abundance elsewhere? The ironic reality is that we actually miss out all the time and cannot have it all. Social media loves to bombard us with a perceived abundance of options. The more we feel that we miss, the more we diminish the chances of ever feeling content with what we do have. How important are the things that we really want? It's a common human trait to be dissatisfied and to focus on what we do not have. This drives our FOMO.

The pain of missing out becomes more significant than what we have not missed. This internal drive has a negative side effect that causes boundless restlessness, envy, and displeasure.

The ancient Greek philosopher and sage Epicurus, born in 341 BC, wisely said "do not spoil what you have by desiring what you have not; remember what you now have was once among the things you only hoped for" (Einzelgänger, 2021). It's encouraging to know that humans from so many centuries ago had similar fears and struggles! The things that we desire so much may be based on an idealized version of reality, and we may have overlooked what really matters and clouded our judgment. We end up paying a high price of collectively chasing the wind and comparing ourselves with peers.

One way to find relief from this senseless chasing is to shift our focus—it may not be easy, but the rewards are great. Shifting focus to what we do have, making a list of things we are grateful for, and being attentive to a thing or an event that outbalanced what we were afraid to miss, ultimately rewrites our perspective. If it is not a disaster to avoid an event, then why did we miss it in the first place? Things may appear as huge, but over time they lose their significance. Take a look from a broader perspective, have a different angle on the topic, and keep a cosmic view of the impermanence and insignificance of things. We often convince ourselves of the importance of social engagements, for example. In doing so, we end up with numerous hangovers, constantly making small talk, faking smiles with people we do not even like or know, filling our social media accounts with pictures, and feeling disappointed when we do not get enough likes on social media. Why do we keep this up? Because we want to belong… If we contemplate the long-term consequences, it makes more sense to create a realistic image. A method called "negative visualization"—that is, making a list of negative aspects associated with what we fear missing out on, and avoiding that—turns FOMO into a victory. "Missing out" then becomes a victory instead of a tragedy over false desires of belonging.

## CONTROL ISSUES

Ironically, control is merely a response to the fear of losing it! This fear is often rooted in the past trauma of being vulnerable and at the mercy of other people. Feeling helpless fabricates the fear and leads to overly controlling behavior. For some individuals, feelings of unpredictability and ambiguity cause control issues. Apart from this, control issues may be rooted in anxiety disorders or other personality disorders. This is why being too clean or organized versus being too messy or disorganized are both sides of the same coin. At the root of the issue lies a deep need to create a sense of safety. A compulsion to micromanage the environment and manage the behaviors of others, or the rigidity with routine rules, cleanliness, and order, eventually results in dysfunctional relationships and maladaptive interpersonal functioning. These controlling responses are often based on unconscious, unacknowledged, and unresolved trauma from an abusive past. Issues with trust, abandonment, fear of failure, perfectionism, and emotional sensitivity drive the controlling behavior.

Ways to counter this are listed below:

- Examine the beliefs that are limiting and driving your behavior: If they do not serve you, let them go.
- Ask yourself what makes you feel afraid.
- Determine the reasons for your nervousness in a particular situation.
- Ground your fears by asking what the worst thing is that could happen in an uncontrollable situation.
- Re-establish your needs and determine if they are being met.

- Educate yourself about anxiety and uncertainty.
- Bring self-awareness to your efforts of control and re-assess them.
- Get support from professionals or outsiders.
- Check your control-oriented language if necessary, and change the language to suit the situation and the people you are talking to.

"You can't control everything, but you can control your attitude and approach to life" (Robbins, n.d.).

## COMFORT NESTS

The first thing that comes to my mind when I think of a comfort nest is the soft cushioned space where we can lie a baby down to rest. I also think of the comforting nest that my cat crawls into on a cold, rainy day, when nothing makes her leave. Then I visualize the space we create for ourselves inside a home, when we feel vulnerable and we need assurance of security and safety. In my house, that room is filled with books and plants. Yes, I admit there are too many books, and the plants have a tendency to propagate themselves. Still—surrounding yourself with comfort items does enhance a feeling of tranquility.

That is exactly why we keep accumulating things that help us feel safe and comforted from the complexities of life. In the same sense as with sentimental cluttering, some people find comfort in surrounding themselves with objects that make them feel safe and happy. A person may not feel well at a specific time and rely on the items to provide a sense of comfort. The healthy directive is to find a balance between simplicity and comfort.

## NUMBING OUT

To feel numb literally means to be immobilized, desensitized, and in shock. Emotionally numb equates to a complete lack of emotion. Most of the time it results from trauma, depression, and unpleasant feelings, and ultimately holds us back from leading healthy and fulfilled lives if it becomes a chronic state of mind. It makes the person feel disconnected from others and sometimes even from themselves, leaving only intense sensations of loneliness, isolation, and confusion. There are multiple causes of emotionally numbing out (PTSD, depression, or depersonalization disorder), but the most obvious one associated with clutter is emotional avoidance—a coping mechanism to push overwhelming emotions aside and not deal with the negativity.

Self-soothing clutter illustrates avoidance and distraction from real problems. The tragedy is that it often results from the suppression of traumatic events. We try to avoid facing the difficult emotions accompanying the stressors. PTSD or trauma responses frequently accompany the loss of a parent or significant other and cause intense trauma that reduces our desire for self-care. In many cases, depressive episodes fuel this further and we fall back on neglecting ourselves and our homes. In some cases, depression may be so severe that people do not go out of their homes at all, compounding the emotional clutter with physical clutter by ordering in meals and becoming more isolated from society. This, then, increases the cycle of embarrassment and loss of control.

The easiest way to healthier coping strategies for numbing out is based on exercise, a healthy diet, regular sleep patterns, and in severe cases, therapeutic treatment and medication. An instantly effective coping mechanism is pressing yourself to interact socially with significant others who are supportive and understanding of your situation.

## HOLDING ON TO MEMORIES

Where is the fine line between reminiscing constructively and remaining stuck in negative nostalgia from the past? Nostalgia is a way of balancing and regulating our emotions, especially when the emotions involve feelings of loneliness, social isolation, and meaninglessness. Reminiscing about the past under these circumstances makes us feel more supported and connected. Nostalgia also has a strong subconscious component, and it has been found that sensory inputs—like cold temperatures, music stimulation, and scent-evoking triggers—have a positive and regulatory function that stimulates physiological comfort. "Zhou et al. (2012) found that nostalgia is triggered by coldness, and in turn predicts an increase in physical warmth" (Stoycheva, 2020).

Reliving the past can certainly uplift the present moment with feelings of connectedness and the meaning of life, but when does it cross the boundary of health? The imbalance appears when the present moment is forsaken for a complete immersion in the past in an attempt to reinstate and glorify the past. This leads to mental health problems and prevents us from using more healthy coping strategies to heal. The hoarding impulse is closely linked to the less healthy nostalgic immersion and often happens without conscious thought until it's too late and the hoarder becomes aware of 'the mess.'

The most effective way to withstand nostalgic impulses is to make the unconscious conscious, and harness the power to function more realistically. Confronting the hurt, shame, and longing from the past is necessary to remove any biased beliefs. Attaching emotional value to objects is a major culprit for cluttering. Most people find it extremely hard to let go of these items. Experts advise putting them in a container (if you absolutely suffer too much from letting them go) and marking that container with a future date for release. Another option is to take photos of the items and then let them go with gratitude. Always enquire about the emotion—ask yourself what you are trying to recreate, if it is helping the present moment, and what you are avoiding.

## THE PROCRASTINATION HABIT

Procrastination is not a serious problem, but it does create serious problems when we do not start things on time! Most people have the tendency to procrastinate at some point in their lives. We do this because we often underestimate the time it will take to complete a project, and overestimate how much time is left, and then this creates a distorted sense of security of the task warranting completion. We also tend to require motivation or inspiration before we attempt a project, but the reality is that the right time never arrives, especially if the task is tedious (like decluttering or organizing) and we end up never completing it.

Depression, Obsessive Compulsive Disorder (OCD), and Attention Deficit Hyperactivity Disorder (ADHD) are the main contributors to procrastination. Self-doubt, lack of energy, worry, maladaptive perfectionism, and distraction are primary culprits that prevent us from taking action when these disorders are the realities of our lives. Others may simply have fairly common reasons for postponing what needs to be done, like forgetting, making a habit of waiting until the last minute before starting, or prioritizing one project over another. We get the dreamer, the perfectionist, the worrier, and the crisis-maker, to name a few types!

There is a difference between healthy procrastination and unhealthy procrastination. Active procrastinators like to feel challenged and enhance their motivation by working under pressure, and therefore delay the task until the last minute. Passive procrastinators generally have trouble making decisions and pulling them through, resulting in delays. Psychologist Piers Steel clarifies the habit by stating,

> People who don't procrastinate tend to be high in the personality trait known as conscientiousness, one of the broad dispositions identified by the Big Five theory of personality. People who are high in conscientiousness also tend to be high in other areas including self-discipline, persistence, and personal responsibility (Cherry, 2020c).

In order to give Dr. Steel's words more context, the five personality traits are the basic personality dimensions as defined by contemporary psychologists: openness, agreeableness, extroversion, neuroticism, and conscientiousness.

The negative impacts of chronic procrastination are more than poor time management, with profound effects on lifestyle and functioning. It negatively affects mental health, social and professional life, financial stability, and well-being. These chronic habits are often accompanied by stress, resentment, and practical consequences. Some of the most efficient ways to manage procrastination and to keep on track with taking action are:

- Make a to-do list with set due dates.
- Break down the list into small, manageable steps to avoid feeling overwhelmed.
- Recognize warning signs and pay attention to resist the urge to procrastinate.
- Eliminate distractions by turning them off or putting them out of sight.
- Reward yourself by indulging in a fun activity when you congratulate yourself on finishing a task.

Another excellent procrastination management technique is called "temptation bundling." This is basically a functional way to maintain healthy habits, even if the temptation to avoid them persists. It has been proven that behavior change results from this. When you pair a good habit that you struggle to maintain (e.g. organizing the house) with a joyful, indulgent habit (e.g listening to a specific podcast show while you organize), it increases healthy habits. Listening to this favorite podcast while cleaning the house may just make you feel better once you have accomplished the task! Finding the perfect match for your unique personality makes the difference that adds value to the dreaded task. Another example is to schedule a weekly cleaning session together while talking to your best friend on the phone. Be mindful to always pair an activity with a habit that will increase productivity, and experiment with strategies to find the best solution for you. Work smarter, not harder!

## IDENTIFY YOUR SPECIFIC ISSUES

It is useful to keep a fears worksheet available in order to identify your fears. There are many online options available, but you can also create a basic framework of questions to ground yourself when you encounter triggers or find yourself in stressful situations. The important thing to focus on is how feelings matter and can be harmful to you and others. Start by making a list of your fears, describe the thoughts surrounding them, determine where any bodily sensations arise when you are talking about them, and then create a plan of action for future prevention. Our thoughts and feelings are linked, and we can increase our awareness of them by identifying their bodily responses. Bodily responses may be trying to communicate to us that we are feeling angry, afraid, sad, and so forth. In this way, we identify our fears, and we can use this awareness to manage them.

# 4

# MENTAL DECLUTTERING

Let go! Give your clutter a meaning; be grateful for its purpose in your past life and let it go to charity where it serves a new purpose. That's the easy part—letting go of physical clutter. When we go deeper into the mental realm of silencing thought clutter, we have to apply mindful attention and energy to the process. So, let's look at ways to create more ease and flow for our minds.

## THOUGHTS AND REALITY

Fear is the primary aspect limiting our beliefs. It is often the progress-blocking fear that needs to be addressed to overcome the limitations of our perception and enhance liberation. This fear is closely related to clutter management because our core beliefs about what we keep in our space, the things we deserve, and our capabilities define our perception of reality. All people have the ability to create and maintain a clutter-free environment, regardless of character and personality traits. We can be left-brain or right-brain oriented, but we still have the ability to create order in the chaos. It is literally a matter of addressing our fear of letting go.

The subconscious is basically a huge database of memories and information that we have collected over our lifespan. It is inside this vast space where our beliefs and perceptions are formed and maintained, and these ultimately influence our experience of the world. When our beliefs are misinterpreted and distorted, it affects our functioning and limits our growth. This unbalanced status quo supports emotions of frustration, mental exhaustion, anxiety, and so forth. But how we see the world depends on us. We always have a choice—sometimes the choice is just a little more complicated to enforce.

### *Faulty Thinking*

Faulty thinking is often based on misinterpretation or poorly translated, unbalanced information. Someone can say something to us and within the context, we make assumptions that are not based on reality. We tend to put words to others' actions that are not in line with their intention or true meaning. A friend may simply have a personal issue with someone else or simply be having a bad day, but we misinterpret a random remark as offensive and personal. The tragedy is that even though we sometimes know we misinterpret the situation or the conversation, our minds still download and keep the information, ensuring it affects us in the future.

Family scenarios and childhood experiences unfortunately often fall in this category and events get poorly translated. These situations condition most of our core beliefs later in life. To correct this, we have to remind ourselves that many of those beliefs are based on a child's perception and interpretation. Children do not always understand the subtext of situations and they take things at face value. A good example of this is when a child tries to impress their mother by tidying up the kitchen (with good intentions of bringing some relief to her busy schedule), only to be reprimanded because something gets broken in the process. The mother's reaction could be based on her external and personal experience of a bad day at work, resulting in her taking out her frustrations on the child. But the conditioning problem starts when the child is unable to interpret the innuendo and starts believing that they are bad at cleaning up. And so the seed is planted that grows into a limiting belief when it comes to organizing clutter.

### *Eyewitness Effect*

Human beings have the magical ability to distort their account of events. This is called "the eyewitness effect," causing information to be biased and misinterpreted. It is mainly based on the fact that unpleasant and emotional events are recalled subjectively and poorly in comparison to neutral events. It is ascribed to the faulty emotional processing that takes place during traumatic events, but stays with the memory of the event, thus making the memory less efficient and flawed. Unfortunately, we tend to remember how and what we would like to remember.

### *Your Mind Is a Tool*

Eckhart Tolle's book *The Power of Now* (1997) focuses on strategies to help the mind calm down. He emphasizes the fact that we often dwell too much on the future and the past, and thus waste our energy on something that we cannot do much about. Instead, we waste our thoughts on incessant mental noise and biased identities that rob us of our enjoyment of life. So, the crux of the matter is to rise above our thoughts in order to find a true sense of calm and ultimately not be enslaved by the mind. Many contemporary therapies focus on rebalancing the power over our minds (instead of allowing the mind to control us) by promoting focused attention to breathing, meditations, bodily sensations, or emotional reactions to specific situations. If we look at the mind this way, it becomes easier to manage a 'tool' than an abstract entity.

### *Thoughts*

Our brain may also over-translate and over-interpret information when we are overwhelmed by the amount of information coming from a specific source. Despite the fact that we correctly interpret the information, our brains are overwhelmed and create an imbalanced perception of the knowledge. This is also called an "echo chamber"—when we continuously send and receive the same information from the same source repeatedly until they make our beliefs biased. We can change our thoughts to be helpful, rather than allowing them to continuously create illusions.

## THOUGHT SPAGHETTI

Where do our thoughts come from? Neurotransmitters create and fire thought formation back and forth in our brains. The problem is that most of our thoughts arise from the subconscious that we generally do not remember. It is said that 95% of our brain activity is happening in the subconscious. This thought is much scarier! Intrusive thoughts are mostly triggered by anxiety and stress or hormonal changes in the body resulting in thought dilemmas. We can call them "thought spaghetti" for the simple reason that they constitute faux pas or embarrassing acts when all the information neurons touch each other and create chaos. Most of these thoughts are not rationally based nor valid, but we still rely on them. Two of the most powerful methods to master them are focusing on the activity and being attentive to mindfulness in the act.

### *Focus*

Focus your attention on acceptance and admit that spending too much time inside your mind has a negative effect on your life that isolates you and makes you anxious. Then, slow down and focus on doing one thing at a time with awareness and attention to the activity. It's like a scanning and checking method during the day to make sure that thoughts contribute meaningfully to your life.

### *Mindfulness*

Be mindful of focusing, and instead of hovering over the same incessant thought, repeat the thought in a different mental language to yourself, allowing it to lose its power. It is much more useful to say "Here is that thought again that makes me believe so and so"—without judgment and interpretation. Ask yourself if the thought matters. If the thought is not useful (you can often determine this by checking in on your muscle tension), let it go and then move on.

## THE NEGATIVE INNER CRITIC

The opposing persona of the nurturing critic inside our heads is the inner critic that has the sole purpose of keeping us safe and giving us behavioral warnings. Although it has a valid function, it can go overboard sometimes and create many negative outcomes. The constant stream of self-destructive thoughts eventually encourages maladaptive behavior and belittles us, all while it undermines positive feelings, goal-directed activities, and our self-worth. Psychologists call it the "negative self-evaluation." It also increases anxiety, kills confidence, and interferes with our performance. The negative inner critic thrives on comparison (leading to a sense of diminished inferiority), personalization (making us believe that everything is about ourselves and only our faults), labeling (creating false and generalized statements about ourselves), and 'should' statements (making us think that we can achieve the impossible and then beating us up when we fail).

Apart from evolution and cultural scripts, the inner voice is mostly influenced by parental conditioning. So, how do we shut it up when it goes overboard? One of the best methods is to take a ten-minute mirror meditation. Sitting in a comfortable space in front of a mirror and looking reflectively at your image externalizes the critic and makes you see the victim of the negative thoughts. Be attentive and notice the thoughts that come to you while you are looking in the mirror. By looking at how hard you can be on yourself, the self-compassion voice comes back spontaneously. It is important to balance the inner critic and the inner nurturer for a less biased decluttering approach.

## COMMON CLUTTER-UPS

"Clutter-ups" are root beliefs you may have about clutter and your stuff. These can hamper your progress, so once you identify your unique style, acknowledge it, silence the inner critic, and fight back! Some of these clutter-ups include:

- I'm a slob.
- I'm just like this.
- I'm disorganized.
- I'm not good enough.
- I need things.
- I am not worthy.
- Decluttering only works for other people.

No! The mess starts when you believe the stigmatized version of the real you. Face your false clutter-ups and manifest a more positive outcome.

## SHIFT ROOT BELIEFS OF CLUTTER

There are five steps to take in the process of reducing limitations and shifting root beliefs. The most difficult step is to identify the limiting belief (or fear) that holds you back from decluttering your space, lifestyle, and mind. The answer often lies in the thoughts you repeatedly echo. If you continuously utter the sentence, "I cannot get the clutter out of my way because it holds too much sentimental value," the limiting belief may be fear of letting go of the past. What if you decide to embrace the present moment instead of holding on to memories? Will you lose something or gain something? Let's think about that for a moment...

After identifying the limiting belief, we can move on to the source of the fear by asking ourselves the question, "where does it come from?" Only through understanding something do we gain knowledge for improvement. It is important to remember that this is not a process of finding someone or something to blame. Blame does not assist with healing and recovery. Reaching an understanding of the root cause is our aim. The third step is to find the reason behind the source. This facilitates empathy and brings compassion, not only to others who were involved in forming the root belief, but also to ourselves. It often opens up the road to better understanding, especially for incidents that were misinterpreted or poorly translated during our childhood.

Introducing the truth to ourselves may be the more difficult fourth step because it is impossible to simply remove a belief unless we replace it with something. This process involves a meeting with our subconscious and the only way to convince our biased memory bank is to bombard it with the undeniable truth that eradicates the old limiting belief. Good inspiration for this is to find hope with other mentors or significant people who demonstrate the possibility that change is indeed possible. Taking small steps with things that we thought were impossible, will assist with breaking through the discomfort and proving that we are capable of the change. This is why an action plan of removing one piece of clutter on a daily basis is so encouraging, as it builds upon the victory from the previous day when we realize that nothing has been lost in letting go! Once you realize you feel better, it serves as encouragement.

Lastly, remember the power of words. Yehuda Berg said that "Words have energy and power with the ability to help, to heal, to hinder, to hurt, to harm, to humiliate, and to humble" (Economy, 2015). They are able to solidify a truth, but the impact of their power remains in your hands. Even if you are having difficulty reaching your goal, the mere expression of your intention drives your thoughts in a more positive direction. Be mindful not to negate all your hard work with a few thoughtless uninspiring words. Rewrite those "I can't" expressions to "I am capable of..." and enjoy the outcome that these words manifest.

## REFRAME YOUR CLUTTER IDENTITY

The legend is told of the students of Socrates who wanted to give him some money to buy a new pair of sandals. They saw him going to the market daily with his old pair and told him that they value his free teaching and would like to show gratitude by giving him the money to buy new sandals. His response was that he was delighted with them, but also delighted with his old sandals. He explained his philosophy of how he likes to go to the market daily to see how many things are being sold that he doesn't need. The moral of this beautiful story is that our wealth is not measured by material things, but rather by the things that money cannot buy. I can live with this truth!

Here are ways to counter some of our clutter identity archetypes:

- The sentimental clutterer should be approached carefully and gently. It is advisable for them to talk to someone about the memory of the item, share the story behind the item, and then let it go. The story will remain and live on without the item. Photos and children's art can even be saved online when taking a photo and saving it, or it can be shared via social media with others for a deeper experience.
- Painful clutter generally includes things like the anger letters after a break-up or the wedding dress after a divorce. These items can gain new meaning by being useful and functional elsewhere. A rewarding option is to donate them as gifts to charity, which gives them much more meaning than hoarding them in a dusty box.
- "Sunk cost fallacy" is best approached when you admit your mistake and let the item go. Don't allow the item to burden your current reality any longer! Saying to yourself that your life has changed or admitting that you don't need the item anymore helps you reach toward freedom. "Sunk cost fallacy" and frugality are often symptoms of a fear of lack in the future, especially financial lack. The real danger for frugal archetypes is that they miss out on enjoying the value of new things in their lives because they refuse to spend money on new items that may enhance their lives while ending up living in a constant mental state of scarcity. It can be overcome by setting a small budget for frivolous spending or an entertainment budget, and also by becoming an antique trader or thrift shop operator where the need will still be fed,

but rewards are more healthy when objects are not being hoarded.

- Identity clutter ties you to some perceived identity. 'Stuff' like maternity clothes or the t-shirt you never wear from that one marathon you ran 20 years ago, are examples of this. The solution is to remind yourself that holding on to the past prevents you from living fully in the present moment. Acknowledge the fact that these things have a hold on you unless you release them, and remember that items do not define your identity, as your identity should not depend on material items.
- Resourceful clutter may be linked to FOMO, fear of lack, and fear of neglect, so this clutterer keeps hanging on to information to the point of the items becoming stale and ironically losing their resourcefulness. These gatherers should acknowledge that life is an endless resource of information, and the 21st century continuously updates our info hub, so there is no need to stack them on a pile that gathers dust. Rather, try to allow the new info in and release the old.

I am also reminded of Michelangelo, who said he saw an angel in the marble and started to remove pieces of the stone and chisel the marble to set the angel free. Isn't living like sculpting, where we have to *remove* in order to enjoy the essential? Many of us identify with acquiring instead of releasing, and we end up feeling worse. Perhaps it's time to adjust our clutter identities when we find ourselves in this space.

## QUICKLY CALM AN UNQUIET MIND

"The art of a simple life begins with shedding" (Itani, 2021). We have to learn to move from multiplicity to simplicity. What is multiplicity? Too many lists to finish, endless distractions, fragmented and conflicting activities, and always seeking more instead of being content with what we have. This all adds to a life of overwhelming multiplicity. It happens when we ignore our own journey and follow the pace set by the crowd, while forgetting our destinies and goals. It happens when we waste our energy on things that do not serve our purpose or nurture the soul. It happens when we try to please other people whose values don't meet ours. It becomes even worse when we complicate our issues with overthinking, drain our valuable resources, and deplete our energy levels.

Sometimes, we spend all our energy on collecting more of everything—memories, things, moments, projects, futile responsibilities, connections, social outings, more holidays, more books to read, and in the end, we have drained all our energy while trying to hold on. Too much consumption has the devastating effect of ironically creating a vast hole filled with the nothingness that makes us feel empty inside. We lose control, our emotions become disorganized, and we have difficulty with our daily functioning, all resulting in reduced productivity. Consumption also has the nasty habit of making us think that we are achieving something when we are in fact just wasting our precious time. It's an illusion, for example, to think that watching endless cooking shows online will help us learn to cook. Getting into the kitchen and actively starting to cook will produce far better results.

It is, therefore, important to understand that our fulfillment is not sustained by consumerism, but rather by creation. Too much of anything burdens the scale and eventually tips it over. We should remind ourselves that choosing three truly valuable elements is more than enough to maintain a simplified life. But we have to start by making the mindful choice of living slowly. And this starts with shedding, letting go of all the things we have outgrown, and the needless possessions that clutter our lives. Shedding includes emotional baggage that drags us down, toxic friends, unwanted burdens, vanity and pride, and selfish egos. It mostly includes the irrational desire to keep busy simply to satisfy our perception of constantly having to do something. Maybe we still harbor childhood misinterpretations or faulty thinking of being 'lazy' when we were simply—and quietly—in the moment of doing nothing. It is time to rewrite that conditioning and allow ourselves to know that it's okay to do nothing sometimes. We do not always have to fill the silent gaps.

Letting go is not a loss, but rather a renewal. In the process, we arrive at our authenticity, our inner selves, and this is only possible if we are not distracted by a multitude of physical and mental clutter that absorbs our energy and steers us away from our purpose.

### *Meditation*

We will look at meditation in depth in Chapter 9. Meditation does not necessarily mean that you find emptiness, silence, or nothingness. It also does not have to take hours. A mere five minutes of mindfully drinking your tea and focusing on the enjoyment of the cup and the flavor of the tea with all your senses is a meditation in itself that brings tranquility. Also, a few simple breathing exercises are useful to quickly calm a restless mind. Here are three easy methods for quick relief from a cluttered and anxious mind:

#### Breathing and Gratitude

- Focus on your breathing and become aware of your state of mind. What does your breath convey about your emotions? Write down the feelings (agitated, energized, grounded, etc.) while you pay attention to your breath.

- List a few things that you are grateful for at the specific moment. It could even be something basic, like having the company of a pet, pleasant weather, or a new friendship. The idea is to focus on gratitude.
- Manifest your day by setting an intention. It could be anything from feeling grounded, remaining calm during challenges, or eating mindfully.
- Lastly, let go by asking yourself what is holding you back that no longer adds value to your life. Make a list of worries or items that drag you down and clutter your environment. It can be something like letting go of trying to be perfect all the time or releasing constant worry.

### STOP

This option creates mental space to help you worry less. The present moment can relieve negative effects of stress and regulate responses to regain perspective. It is called the "STOP technique," which follows:

- *Stop* what you are busy with.
- *Take* three deep abdominal breaths.
- *Observe* your feelings, thoughts, emotions, posture, and bodily sensations by understanding that they are impermanent (by naming emotions, we reduce fear circuits in the brain and induce calmness).
- *Proceed* with an activity that supports you better in the present moment (have a cup of tea, go for a walk, journal).

By tuning into your feelings and emotions, you are able to change perspective.

## Letting Go

Learning to identify limiting and inaccurate stories you tell yourself is liberating. Create a new story by practicing true reflection of the stories you believe about yourself.

- Find a tranquil place to do this reflection.
- Question the stories and find out what makes them hold you back from joy.
- Determine what you would really want in your life. You can do this by imagining yourself when you introduce yourself to a stranger.
- Now, focus on how the limiting story makes you feel and how your body responds to this emotion. What thoughts come to mind while you think of this story of yourself?
- Then, check its validity and accuracy. Start by imagining how it would feel if you didn't believe the story. Experience the 'what if' moment of letting go. What will you lose if you let it go?
- Consider what was holding you back and how you would do things differently if you did not believe the story. Continue checking what parts of the story hold you back from improvement.
- Observe the new feeling, then let the old story go. Be compassionate and patient with yourself. Letting go in bite-size chunks is better than never letting go of stories past their 'sell-by date.'

### *Mental Calmness Exercises*

Scientific research has found that a mere 45-minutes of creativity can lower anxiety and stress because it lowers the cortisol levels in your body. Even if you are not artistically inclined, your body will respond favorably to focused creative activity. We become more mindful of the present moment, leaving us fulfilled, raising our confidence levels, creating an emotional release, and producing higher self-esteem.

When we have reached a point in our lives where we fell into the trap of too much consumption and overwhelming responsibilities, creativity can be one of the most effective ways to buffer exhaustion and inactivity. Mihály Csíkszentmihály writes in his book *Flow: The Psychology of Optimal Experience* (1990) that a mindful immersion in activity creates a state of flow. In his words,

Flow is a state in which people are so involved in an activity that nothing else seems to matter; the experience is so enjoyable that people will continue to do it even at a great cost, for the sheer sake of doing it (Itani, 2021a).

The truth of this remark is underlined with the word "enjoyable." There is a difference between enjoyment and pleasure. Passive activities like eating and sleeping create pleasure, but active experiences that demand our focused attention (like sports, art, writing) create much more immersion in joy. They are mostly rooted in creation, not in consumerism. I remember my professor once said that the success of the art of writing depends on you remaining seated on the chair. Now, that is quite a powerful statement of focused immersion in the present moment! And it has proved itself to me as a highly productive and very enjoyable activity in my life. Research proved that our heart rates slow down and breathing normalizes when thoughts are absorbed by a focused activity. What makes it even more worthwhile is the visual reward of our creation and a feeling of accomplishment toward the end of the activity. This creates calmness and harmony.

### *Activities That Provide Focus*

We often overlook the value of simple daily activities and

mental reminders that provide focus to our challenging lives. Consider the following:

- Chores – doing your daily maintenance chores with focused awareness provides calmness.
- Routines – following a healthy routine that provides nourishment for your mind and body anchors strength.
- Setting goals – identifying just a few goals and giving them your devoted attention guarantees success.
- Finding a decluttering method and then sticking to it – whether you have to declutter physical, digital, relational, or mental space; the Keep It Simple Stupid rule (K.I.S.S.) always applies to maintain it effortlessly. Find the most simple, unique method that works for you, and keep doing it!

Change can be daunting, but it can also be liberating when we face and acknowledge the truths about ourselves behind the intended change.

# 5

# EMOTIONAL DECLUTTERING

We might clutter up our lives to avoid facing difficult thoughts and feelings. Until we face and process them, we will remain stuck.

## WHY WE NEED EMOTIONS

Emotions have a variety of purposes in our lives and give us the necessary resources for meaningful interaction. They can be quite powerful, tenacious, complex, and life-changing. So, why do we need them? Apart from making us understand each other better, they also make us take action, avoid danger, and gain motivation. We clearly need to face and understand them in order to improve our lives. Emotions not only have a psychological component, but they affect our physical reactions and behaviors.

Motivations produce emotions. Extrinsic motivation is reward-driven from an exterior source (running a race to win the cup) and intrinsic motivation is driven by internal desires to find personal reward and enjoyment (reading a book to increase knowledge). Each type has a different outcome, but the latter generally holds a more positive kind of emotion. Extrinsic motivation implies an expectation, while intrinsic motivation automatically rewards personal choice since the activity is the inherent reward. One is not better than the other, but they both carry different values. Every situation and personality type requires a different approach, and this is why we need to understand them.

Our motivations determine our desired outcomes with decluttering. Are we tidying up to impress someone else, or are we making a deliberate choice to tidy up because we prefer a more simplified and organized lifestyle? These questions reach into our feelings, identify them, face them, work with them, and ultimately help us to achieve our goals. Let's explore emotions a bit more—what are emotions?

### *Messengers of Inner Health*

When we analyze our emotions and reflect on their origin, they help us make informed decisions that positively impact our health. Not only do they tell other people what we need, but they also inform us. Of course, in a moment of rage, we may not be as aware of the emotional message as our onlooker who's watching our facial expression. But when mindful reflection follows an emotional outburst, we often find solutions or reasons for the underlying emotion. Emotions talk to us this way and inform us that change is needed or that something deserves our attention. Thus, even negative emotions have a useful message to convey that we learn from to develop.

### *Avoiding Our Feelings*

Avoiding our emotions and bottling them up has no positive outcome. Ignoring them simply makes them come back repeatedly, and when we feel overwhelmed or stressed out by something else, these snubbed emotions take revenge when we react mindlessly. We also rob ourselves of any opportunities for growth, introspection, understanding, and improvement if we avoid emotions. When we feel angry, there is probably a good reason why we feel the emotion. Sadness may be indicating a loss of some kind. Did we lose our dream? Did we miss out on a good opportunity? Or did we overfill our lives to the point where we are constantly feeling overwhelmed? When we stop ignoring emotions and break down their components by asking ourselves these questions, we establish the root cause of their screaming—we listen and improve.

### *Taking Action and Making Decisions*

Emotions drive our fight-or-flight responses. We tend to take action to avoid negative emotions and increase positive emotions. In some cases, an anxious emotion can create a positive outcome, for example, feeling a little stressed before an interview, presentation, or exam. In these cases, the emotion does not only increase the likelihood of taking action, but also enhances the performance. It has also been found that experiencing joy motivates action.

Our emotional perception of an event, person, or circumstance can assist us with making informed decisions that lead to change. Emotional intelligence plays a crucial role in all areas of our lives, and it has been proven that people with dysfunctional emotional intelligence (the inability to understand and manage emotions) have related decision-making inabilities. If we apply this powerful driving ability of our emotions to the decluttering activity, the outcome can only produce success.

## WORKING WITH EMOTIONS

If you are not happy with your home environment and have to answer the question "Should I find another home?" or "Should I be more grateful for what I already have?" you have reached step one. The improvement process starts with identifying the root issue. Everybody has unique ways to deal with emotions; some do introspection while others rely on outdoor recreational activities. Problems arise when we do not address them. We deny ourselves inner peace if we ignore them. Yes, it is good to be able to cope with whatever life throws our way, remain strong in any situation, or resolve our internal issues about a specific problem—but sometimes the problem is not us. Rather, it is, in fact, the environment that needs to change. In many unhealthy situations, we tend to focus on changing ourselves. We do not analyze the scenario and end up beating ourselves up about it when, truly, we have put ourselves in a really difficult situation! Sometimes, some meditation skills and a few breathing exercises will not bring true comfort to an extreme situation and still leave our irritable nerves on edge all the time. So, what is the solution? There are ways to modify an environment that is more conducive to mental strength. These include:

- Ask yourself if you need to change the situation or your feelings about the situation. Work with a plan in mind. Merely changing the perception of the situation is sometimes the key to tranquility, health, and mental strength.
- Make good habits easy to access so that when you encounter a slight challenge, it's easier to change course. This way, you set yourself up for long-term success.
- Make unhealthy habits difficult to access. You do not have to be strong enough to cope with everything. Create distance between you and your unhealthy habits. Keep the cookie pot in an inaccessible top-shelf position! You will have more energy to remain focused.

- Be mindful of who you allow into your life. People around you affect your mental health and stability. It is crucial to establish boundaries and start saying "no." Emotions and behaviors have a huge impact on you, so manage them mindfully!
- Manage your physical environment. Put your phone away, ignore the digital pressure of social media, and the unhealthy demands on your lifestyle. Remove the clutter from your desk because it simply adds to your stress. Organizing your space makes you feel calmer. It has been found that even the color of walls can drain your energy. Stay focused on building more inner strength and harmony.

### *Identifying Emotions*

Emotions have three components: the subjective experience, the physiological response, and an expressive component that evaluates the behavioral response. "Research has found that experiencing fear increases perceptions of risk, feeling disgusted makes people more likely to discard their belongings, and feeling joy or anger causes people to leap into action" (Cherry, 2020b). Because we use our emotions to make important decisions for taking action, we have to be able to identify them. For this reason, our emotional intelligence counts because even when we think we make a rational decision that isn't influenced by our feelings, research has proved the opposite.

Emotional demonstrations like body language and facial expressions also give clues for identification. We all remember the face of silent disgust at our chaotic teenage room when our mother opened the door! And when we think of that summer holiday and the first stolen kiss behind the tree, we all still remember the emotions that surged inside our bodies. Emotions speak through our senses—this is how we identify them. Identifying and reading their language helps us to build meaningful relationships and allow effective social communication.

### *Looking for the Need*

When we consider the evolution of man, we are made aware of how emotions evolved over millennia to impact society in many ways. Humans have found ways to survive because of these ways, but the same emotions that ignited the fight, flight, or freeze reaction in the wild are not always useful (nor socially acceptable) in the 21st century. Of all the species, human beings are the most self-conscious, making us innovative survivors. This ability also pushed us up to the top of the food chain because we added a reasoning element to our emotions. We can rationalize the past and future to be more innovative in the survival game.

The problem is that these two abilities have to be balanced for healthy functioning, and this is seldom the reality. Excess emotion fuels many mood disorders and psychological problems in modern-day society. A fast-paced world places more pressure on these jumpy emotions just sitting there without a safe outlet. Fight-or-flight doesn't always cope well with a constant financial crisis or a war situation, and emotions become overwhelming. We surely need them, we cannot escape them, but it has become crucial to process them well.

### *Processing Them*

Built-up emotions are mental clutter that disrupts. We all know the impact of "emotional baggage"—we can only move away from an emotion once we process it. "In psychology, we think of the true self as the part of us that we are born with that is naturally open, curious, and trusting, while the false self emerges as a set of adaptive strategies to deal with pain and loss" (Ishler, 2021). The problem is that the false self doesn't want the true self to express itself, and our trapped emotions remain stuck. Our nervous system tells us what emotion is. If the emotional intensity is high, it can become trapped, and we usually feel this in bodily responses. That 'tightness around your chest' feeling is screaming at you for release.

Repressed emotions and unconscious avoidance wreak physical and psychological havoc with our systems. Some ways to process and release them are to acknowledge them, work through trauma (especially with shadow work), become still (as with meditation, creative tasks, or simply sitting), and focused movement (like yoga, stretching, breathing exercises, or walking meditation).

## IDENTIFYING STRESS TRIGGERS

Some of the most common stress triggers are financial problems, parenting issues, work demands, relationship difficulties, feelings of being overwhelmed and too busy, and some personality traits. The triggers that have an impact on one person may not affect another because the complexities of stress are related to our individual past experiences and conditioning influences. Apart from environmental triggering, past trauma may compound the emotion and behavioral response. What may be a mild inconvenience for me may be a nightmarish experience for another person. Today, I may be able to cope with the ant trail that strings along to the sugar in my kitchen cupboard, but tomorrow, I may be ready to declare war against them.

Financial triggers cause the most significant stress in the USA, according to the American Psychological Association (APA). Research in 2015 reported percentages between 72%–77% of money-related anxiety (Elizabeth Scott, 2019). These stressors are often accompanied by arguments with significant others, 'fear of the mailman,' guilt feelings about wasting money, and general worry about future finances. These distressful emotions also bring up physical and psychological issues. Add some relationship conflict and throw in a couple of teenagers in the picture and we are overwhelmed already before the day starts and we have to face the drama and demands of type A personalities at the office.

Some of the many typical stress identifiers are:

- not making time for pleasurable activities
- poor time management
- absenteeism from school or work
- anger
- social isolation
- panic attacks
- gastrointestinal issues
- anxiety
- losing motivation
- overthinking
- sensitivity to criticism
- mood swings
- defensiveness
- irritability
- frustration
- diminished confidence

Addressing symptoms of stress by following its behavioral patterns when they are triggered, creates more peace of mind. Ignoring them and bottling them up do not contribute to well-being and only lead to additional stress.

## FACING FEARS

Fears steal our lives. They prevent us from enjoying the present moment and they stall our progress. Just like we cannot avoid our emotions, we cannot ignore our fears. Some ways to unpack and calm them center around stress reduction techniques, self-compassion, finding meaningful support, exercise, making deliberate attempts at introducing positive emotions to our lifestyle, and finding a purpose in life. Being in nature has proven its benefits across various scientific fields and cultures, and adding an aerobic element to being in nature doubles up on the feel-good experience.

Traumatic experiences that involve loss of some kind often leave survivors questioning their feelings of guilt and the meaning of their lives. Finding purpose in life after trauma re-establishes a sense of security. In this way, we can prevent fears from hampering our enjoyment of life after stressful life-changing events. Some humor and positivity go a long way in combating fear. Making an attentive effort to find positivity and laughter in your world steers your focus away from the fears that prevent you from living. The Vietnamese Buddhist monk and peace activist Thích Nhất Hạnh said that "Every time your fear is invited up, every time you recognize it and smile at it, your fear will lose some of its strength" (Delagran, 2016).

## THE PAST

The past can have a devastating effect on our well-being. Book shops and the internet are rife with self-help and guidance books about the topic. Podcasts and YouTube videos clutter our digital world, and even Granny has to give her two cents worth of the topic when we meet for weekly tea. Bad things happen to all of us, and as we move through life's journey, we learn along the way. We gather information, make new friends who show support, and let go of things that do not serve us. It is an innate human nature to improve ourselves and our environments. But, sometimes, it is just a little more difficult because our emotions get in the way of the daunting tasks. How can we address the past (because we cannot eliminate it) in order to find some healing and strength? How do we speed up the recovery process so that we feel safe and whole again?

### *Turning Around Past Trauma*

Understanding trauma and its effects on the human system is necessary in order to heal. Trauma is the psychological result of events that shatter, disrupt, and sometimes threaten our safety and security. It inadvertently affects our daily functioning and bodily responses. It makes us feel helpless. Some of the typical symptoms of trauma are upsetting memories that linger, including anxiety, sleeplessness, depression, disconnectedness, issues with trust, being overwhelmed, feeling isolated, helplessness, and a general feeling of numbness. It is not so much the event itself that creates the issue, but the person's subjective response to the trauma that creates the stress.

Trauma can be caused by a one-time event, ongoing relentless stressful events, and even by causes that are generally overlooked. Bullying, childhood neglect, childhood abuse, a violent incident, physical attack, burglary, humiliating and shaming experiences, a break-up with a significant other, sudden death, and especially an event that involved cruelty in some way all form the basis of erratic traumatic responses. Even the bombardment on social media and news pages of violent disruptions can contribute to our experience of the horror of events and present new challenges for us to cope with.

Childhood trauma often has a long-lasting and highly disrupting effect when it is not resolved. It creates helplessness and fears that continue into our adult lives and disrupt all our interactions, often feeding further trauma. The result of prolonged exposure to childhood trauma where the individual experienced continuous feelings of helplessness and the inability to escape from the situation, is Complex Post Traumatic Stress Disorder (CPTSD). The effect of CPTSD is deeply hampering and affects healthy functioning across many areas of life. Only through identification and understanding of the triggering trauma, can the conditioning be addressed and improved. Unless the childhood trauma is resolved, the individual carries over the sense of fear and unsafety into adult life and it permeates all connections and behaviors.

The important thing to remember about trauma is that we all respond differently to traumatic events. Emotional response to trauma can last a few days or months and gradually fades over time. But a traumatic trigger can turn into PTSD when the emotion associated with the trauma persists and causes severe functioning issues. When a person experiences a feeling of being stuck, constantly having psychological shock, and the inability to stabilize emotions, or make sense of the traumatic event in a rational way—PTSD should be addressed with the help of a professional therapist. With the correct guidance, the individual can learn to trust and connect with other people again and regain emotional balance. The most important thing to understand is that your emotional response is normal and valid and that the trauma was what was abnormal, not you.

Dealing with traumatic events always implies loss of some form. The trauma does not necessarily have to involve death or a person. We may feel intense loss over a work opportunity that didn't materialize. A natural grieving process should follow and not be suppressed. Researchers have found that people who ignore this process and avoid facing the trauma end up having more difficulty moving on, resulting in more profound dysfunctional habits.

Let's look at some effective ways of moving through the grieving process of trauma toward recovery.

### Releasing Regrets

That moment when you realize you did something that may result in some kind of loss or damage to a relationship or opportunity, and you know you will not be able to repair the consequences —this is an instance of action creating a reaction. We all have these moments, and even though they can be quite distressing, we can always depend on the fact that they actually may open up new doors for change. Perhaps the benefit you wanted or believed you had was not the benefit that life intended for you. The reality is that eventually, you will let go and release the regret from hampering your present peace of mind. The key to a less cluttered mind is to let these emotional regrets go before they become too overwhelming. Ultimately, the action of releasing regrets remains an important initial step to a more meaningful and fulfilling life.

How do we let go of regrets? Some comments from online sources made by individuals focus on replacing regret with something positive. Some people focus on breathing, for instance. We can also trust time to heal the memory and release the emotion. Most people think that every feeling has a purpose, and spending too much time regretting them or reminiscing about them eliminates the lesson we learn from them and robs us of our tranquility. "Feel it, review it, learn it, shed it" (Deschenne, 2010). However we cope with releasing regrets, it always includes facing and resolving the painful feelings and memories associated with the trauma. The blame game does not work with regrets.

### Letting Go

Blaming almost always has negative effects and no positive

outcome. It simply reduces compassion and rekindles hatred, anger, and resentment. By blaming others (or ourselves), we enhance the toxic side effects of our victimhood, rendering us powerless. On the other hand, research has proved that letting emotions go with gratitude generates more positive results. By recognizing and acknowledging our blessings and things that give us moments of joy, we build a strong power base for letting past emotions go, instead of holding on to memories that do not serve us. Gratitude journals, regular short morning meditations, a gratitude jar that you fill with words of blessings, or volunteering all provide immeasurable benefits. Actively pursuing these can release negative fight-or-flight energies and help you rebuild your trust in people by letting go of the fears that trigger emotions.

When you do get stuck with letting go, some useful tips are:

- Check-in with your current emotion.
- Be mindful of its presence.
- Acknowledge the emotion.
- Create a definite separation from the emotion by stepping back.
- See your emotion outside of you as a wave that comes and goes.
- Don't block the emotion and don't ignore it.
- Don't increase the emotion, but simply witness the feeling.
- Remember that you are not the emotion.
- Don't act on the emotion's urge.
- Remind yourself of different emotions.
- Notice other feelings that arise as you look at the emotion from the outside in.

### Working Through Severe Emotional Pain

The best way to balance emotional pain is by regulating emotions. Because emotions are linked with bodily responses, this naturally implies that any physical intervention will be beneficial to restoring balance. Four basic actions to take after trauma are:

- Get moving – mindfulness and exercise restore the unbalanced equilibrium of your bodily functions. They burn adrenaline, release endorphins, and get you out of your hyperarousal state. Any rhythmic 30-minute exercise like running or swimming is beneficial. Focus on being mindful of your bodily movement, use your senses, and feel the wind on your skin or your feet touching the ground. Be aware of your rhythmic breathing. Stay focused on keeping your body safe. Avoid mind chatter while you do this!
- Do not isolate – your natural response after trauma is to disengage and withdraw from social interaction. Try to avoid this as it only makes the grieving process worse. You do not have to talk about the trauma while you engage with a trusted and supportive friend, as the mere act of engaging with someone else has healing benefits. Reconnect with an old friend, become a volunteer, join a support group, or make new friends as long as you actively engage with other people. I have found the healing power of volunteering for animal welfare useful. It's a wonderful way of challenging your feelings of helplessness when you experience the act of helping other vulnerable ones.
- Regulate your nervous system – remember that no matter how traumatized you are, you are always able to regain control and a sense of calm. Allow your feelings to

be, practice mindful breathing, hold on to sensory inputs, and stay grounded. Don't ignore your feelings, acknowledge them because they help you recover. A quick 60-second mindful breathing session where you keep your attention focused on each out-breath brings immediate results and restores calm in your body. Soothe sensory inputs with music, stroking a pet, or whatever quick stress-relief method you prefer. A very grounding (and simple) activity is to sit in a chair and place your feet firmly on the floor, then feel your back against the chair, and find six objects in your environment with blue or red in them. You will immediately feel your breathing settle.

- Take care of your health – a healthy body assists in healthy recovery from trauma. Enough quality sleep is crucial to your health. Maintaining a well-balanced diet consisting of regular small meals is very beneficial. Try to include omega-3 elements like salmon or walnuts and avoid too much sugary and fried food in order to help against mood swings. Lastly, focus on activities that reduce your stress, especially ones that bring you joy. It can be something like yoga, caring for houseplants, a hobby, or even a simple breathing meditation.

## USE EMOTIONAL ENERGY WISELY

Keep in mind the saying "what you resist persists," and always be attentive to grounding yourself. Emotions are there for a good reason and we simply have to learn how to channel them into constructive choices. Emotional decluttering removes the stuff that steals our quality of life. It's up to you to manage this energy wisely.

6

# PHYSICAL DECLUTTERING

The outside world is an extension of our inner world, and vice versa. By sorting out the external, we positively transform the internal. Physical decluttering may be the easiest part, although it may require copious amounts of energy to maintain motivation. A good idea is to take before and after photos as a reminder when you lose hope or when you experience a short relapse. Keep your focus on what can be decluttered today. Make the choice. Take the step. Take action. Feel relief.

## WHAT WOULD YOU TAKE TO SPACE?

Remember that mental, physical, calendar, digital, and relational spaces are all exposed to cluttering. Limiting our obligations makes time for more important things. Simplifying our life creates time, space, energy, and ultimately tranquility.

### *What You Need Versus What You Want*

If you have ever been in a position to travel and had to limit yourself with your packing, you'll understand the difference between things that you really need versus the things you just want. We all try to cram that last item into the suitcase and ask our child to sit on top of it so we can force it closed. On the other hand, you always have that one family member who travels too light and ends up borrowing things from you because they didn't pack their own version of it! So, how do we find a balance between our needs and desires? I ask myself about the value and usefulness of the items. How often will I use it? Is it easily replaceable? Will it be financially viable to replace an item if I do not have it with me? Will I be able to rent or borrow the item temporarily? By asking these simple questions, we quickly discover the difference between a true need and something we can do without.

### *The True Value of Stuff*

The travel technique also applies to our physical space. The magical number of threes comes in very handy here. Three pairs of underwear mean one in the wash, one in the wardrobe, and the other on the *derrière*. And rotate! Do we really need all those pairs of black shoes? An effective decluttering habit is to keep a container in a room where you place all the items that you find challenging to part with, keep them in there for a week (while you add more daily), and then only keep the things that you remember you put inside! This is a good indicator of an item's value and usefulness. You will be surprised at the amount of stuff that we forget about.

## AREAS TO DECLUTTER

Our physical clutter areas include rooms, things, relationships, lifestyles, and schedules. To declutter these, we have to become mindful of self-care. Many of us were conditioned in childhood to avoid selfish behavior. Society prescribes additional emphasis on being less self-absorbed. As a result of faulty thinking, parental conditioning, and societal demands—we end up ignoring our personal need for tranquility. It's time to realize that self-care implicates compassion for others and it's not a negative trait. When we take the time to manage and nurture ourselves wisely, we have more time available to spend with others.

### *Rooms*

A good way to start organizing cluttered rooms is to look at them with a new eye. Imagine being a visitor and visualize the 'visitor eye' as a friend seeing the room for the first time. Ask yourself what your friend would see and say, and then implement that. Your friend's eye would probably see the beautiful room hiding behind all that stuff! They would say how the room is breathing with a fresh look when some items are removed and others creatively organized. The room is just waiting for you to see it. Apply a designer color coding and minimalistic approach to rearrange the furniture, and you should be halfway there!

### *Things*

Some tips to prevent items from becoming cluttered stuff are:

- Check duplicates – always remove the old item after an upgrade. When you accidentally buy something you already have, give away or donate the additional item.
- Identify items that you have not used within one year and let them go. Avoid keeping things for a mere probability. Perhaps you may *not* need them in the future!

- Take a big garbage bag and walk through your house while you fill the bag as fast as possible with items that you can release.

### *Lifestyles and Schedules*

Our hectic schedules affect our lifestyles on every level. Keeping our focus on compassionate self-care relieves us from unnecessary demands and neglected relationships. Not only do we have to declutter our physical spaces, we definitely need to look at managing our time and attention wisely for a more healthy lifestyle (more of this later).

## WHERE TO START

It's wise to remind yourself that smaller tasks make you feel that you have accomplished something. Try not to take on too much at one time, as this may only hamper your motivation to complete the project. Break bigger tasks down into bite-size chunks and reward yourself with a pat on the shoulder (or a glass of champagne!) after each accomplishment. By starting with baby steps, removing one thing daily, and keeping only the things that truly add value to your life, you generate inspiration for future action. You will soon discover that the more action you take, the more it encourages action, and so the cycle feeds itself until you find harmony.

## WHAT SHOULD STAY VERSUS WHAT SHOULD GO

Caroline Rogers focused her master's research on applied positive psychology and coaching psychology on a particular investigation into the relationship between well-being and clutter. In her coaching practice, she introduces the method of imagining a space without clutter. She calls it the "miracle question," and the method involves breathing in through your nose and out through your mouth, closing your eyes while you sit comfortably, and imagining the particular challenging clutter space. Imagine going to sleep, and while you are sleeping, a miracle happens that changes the area to exactly how you need it to be. Open your eyes, notice what you see in your head, experience what you feel, and be mindful of what has happened. Then, stay with the image for some time while you anchor it.

Positive psychology focuses on 'what is' and not 'what isn't.' If you can visualize what you want to see happen and then add the purpose of the space to enhance the visualized image, you'll know what to lose and what to keep. Some useful advice from Marie Kondo is to always greet the space that you plan to tidy up with a mindful intention of turning it into something better and more useful. Taking a moment before you start rearranging a room, wardrobe, packing spaces, or even your computer mailbox brings tremendous focus and direction.

## PRACTICAL ACTIVITY

An efficient way to start decluttering is to have a "packing party" where you invite family members or a group of friends to help you. Two options work well: You can either pretend that you are moving and ask them to help you organize and pack all your belongings into boxes, at which point you only unpack the necessary stuff from those boxes. The rest can receive your gratitude and be given to charity to serve a new purpose. The second option is to engage with a friend (or two) to lose one thing at a certain hour of the first day, two things at the same hour the next day, three items the following day, and so forth for one whole month. Then, you have a celebration party on the 30th day of the month to compare the progress. I think it is quite challenging to find 29 things in one day that you have to remove from your life before you are able to celebrate! Try to focus on collectibles, decor, and kitchen utensils. Donate, recycle, or sell them. If you are ready to take up the challenge, here is a helpful declutter checklist:

- The spare buttons that you keep just in case.
- Out-of-date vouchers and expired credit cards.
- Things that you do not like to look at in your home.
- Clothes that do not fit you anymore, or socks with holes.
- Books—the ones you have never read and probably never will.
- Old diaries and yesteryear calendars.
- Magazines from last year and before!
- Anything that provides information that can be found online when needed.
- Old linen and towels.
- Baby items when your babies are all grown up!
- Cutlery and crockery that are damaged, chipped, and cracked.
- Food that has lived past its expiry date.
- Unfinished projects and crafts that will not be completed.
- The 'bottom of your handbag' stuff.
- Earrings and socks without partners.
- Ornaments that keep gathering dust.
- Memorabilia and expired cards from former celebrations.
- To-do lists of the things you should have done before!
- If you don't remember that it is there, it is time to let it go.

Another useful guide for decluttering is to imagine your 'future self' and set an intention to get there. A concrete decluttering plan based on the 'if/then' concept will help you to bypass your emotional state while taking action toward your goal. You may, for example, say to yourself, "If I feel depressed, I will still sort out the room for five minutes," as opposed to thinking that you have to spend a whole hour tidying up. It helps you to disengage from your emotion about the objects and to focus on the goal.

## ORGANIZING PHYSICAL ENVIRONMENTS

### *Systems*

Having and maintaining systems to organize your things are the most fool-proof prevention against cluttering. When things have a place to go and all cohabitants are aware of this, a well-managed storage system will keep your home (and mind) minimalistic and harmonious. Everything in your home must have a home of its own. A basket in the wardrobe for unruly socks, trays in the kitchen cupboards to keep utensils organized, and bathroom caddies holding all the beauty products will contribute to order! Utilize space wisely and creatively. The area under the bed does not have to become a hoarding paradise that even the cat avoids.

To help you find stuff quickly and know what you have, keep these tips in mind:

- Label containers to avoid messing them up again when you look for something.
- Organize items that match together in groups.
- Color or texture code boxes inside wardrobes, kitchen cupboards, storage spaces, or garages.

### *Decluttering Bins*

Keep four decluttering maintenance bins available for things that you want to remove. These could be:

- To sell – some quality items may still be useful and have value, so consider selling them online or at the local second-hand dealer.
- To donate – those 'over their sell-by-date items' which still look fairly good and can be used by someone else may just be the perfect thing for the charity shop.
- To recycle – let's all improve our green footprint and recycle or upcycle what we can to save the planet.
- To chuck – some poor items have served you well enough and it's time for them to go with gratitude and kindness...

A useful way is to schedule a monthly bin management day for the actual release of these items. Don't bring them back into your home!

## RESTRUCTURING YOUR SPACE

Have a plan. Have scheduled times for implementing your plan. And prioritize the organizing. To restructure your space you have to visualize a goal and purpose. If you know where you are heading, your decluttering process will run smoothly. Try to imagine *what* you want to achieve, and *why* you want to achieve it. Take the time to work through your 'whats' and 'whys' in every room and find out how a decluttered space will impact your life. Asking *why* continuously will keep you focused on the purpose of your goal during those difficult decluttering moments. It is important to stay with this motivation during the whole process. Your purpose is to want the end goal of simplicity so badly that you will be able to work through the rough times.

When you think of what you want to achieve for each room, it is also important to think of the ambiance you would like to create for people who enter your space. Appearance is not only managing a look, but also a feeling. Be realistic about the balance between the creativity and functionality of a room's appearance. A home with children has different requirements from a home with a single occupant. You can also use decorating and design pages to help you visualize the end result, always keeping in mind what you already have and what needs to be replaced. A vision board or some digital apps are all useful to assemble your collage, and they can be a physical reminder of your goal, as well as a motivation to stay focused and mindful about what you buy.

Here are five questions to ask yourself before entering and decluttering each room:

- What is the present function of the room?
- What should the function be?
- How does it feel inside the room?
- What and where are the 'clutter magnets' inside the room?
- What must be done to reach the clear goal for the specific room?

Now that you have your vision, you can create your planning, and start decluttering the things that do not meet the picture in your mind. It may even be a simple vision, like being able to open the window, sit on the couch and read a book, or invite friends over. In this way, you reach your goal easily. Celebrate your victories while you maintain a mindful assessment of your habits to prevent accumulation again.

### *Possessions*

Russel Belk wrote in a research paper in 1988 about the "extended self and possessions," where he highlighted that we see material items as extensions of ourselves, almost like a contagion, which makes it tricky to let them go. A good example is not letting a gift go because we think we have to let go of the person. This is a similar emotion to the one a child has to an attachment toy that they dread losing. It is based on our desire to want to hold on to goodness. Consider what the cause and meaning are of the attachment, as well as for having an attachment to the item. When we determine the correlation between the item and attachment, we tend to make a more informed decision about letting go.

So, with decluttering, the important questions to ask are "Does this item still represent me?" and "Do I still want it in my life?" Understanding the meaning helps work out the meaningfulness. Consumerism and promotional advertising look at the significance of possessions which makes us buy more. It's a challenge to ignore them, and therefore setting up rules as a counter to this consumeristic onslaught is important. What if someone gives you a gift that you do not like, but you still keep because of the extension attachment? Challenge the rule by asking yourself if you gave a gift to someone else and they did not like the gift if you would want them to be burdened by it. Surely the same rule applies to yourself!

The positive psychology approach in terms of our possessions focuses firstly on taking a character strength approach. To identify character strengths, we have to determine "What is quintessentially *me*?" Then, we challenge ourselves by asking how we can apply it to the difficult task (e.g. clutter). Secondly, we focus on mindfulness by training our brains to pay attention. We notice the sensory input, emotions, thoughts that enter our heads, rules, and negative use of the word "should" when we decide about letting go. Being more mindful about the attention paid to a challenge like decluttering the garage, the easier the action becomes.

*Storage Spaces*

The secret to managing storage is minimizing. If you run out of space in one storage area, it does not mean acquiring another storage space! It simply means reducing. Storage spaces should be organized well with functional and easily identifiable containers. Storage facilities' statistics are shocking. According to storage-cafe.com and self-storage trends, there are currently more than 50,000 self-storage units available in America. This is more than double the number of subways and more than three times the number of McDonald's outlets. One-quarter of this percentage is based on customers who do not have enough storage space at home. Furniture and clothing make the top of the storage list. The average rental payment for the most popular units varies between $132-$150 per month. "In 2021 alone, almost 44.8 million rentable square feet were finalized, an area that would cover either the whole of Central Park or the Grand Central Terminal" (Storage-Cafe, 2022). I rest my case.

*Personal Spaces*

Your work desk is probably the personal space that meets you most of the day. It also becomes an outlet for all our emotions. Some days we find it hard to see the photo frames that are supposed to remind us of significant others who really matter. The not-so-urgent folders and to-do lists pile up in one corner, and the plant needs water. The tax-return file lurks on the other corner of the desk and glares at you every time you start a new project. Our emotional outlets read like a book on the desk—frustration, procrastination, neglect, no time for compassion and care, anxious demands, mental saturation, and depression.

But there is always hope! Decluttering and organizing personal spaces should be prioritized exactly because we spend lots of time there. I take a two-options restructuring approach to this. Sometimes it's best to maintain the space constantly by avoiding accumulation. This means attention to prioritizing, tackling, and resolving every new aspect (or item) that arrives at the desk immediately. In this way, we keep the order, and the plant is happy. Option two happens occasionally when there are truly too many things to focus on (I call this "crisis management"). Then, I let go for one day while I prioritize from A to Z according to importance. On these days, I still end the day by tidying up, minimizing, and organizing the desk back to its former order for the next day. My plant is also happy about this and therefore willing to wait until the morning for its drop of water. I have found that if I keep fewer items on my desk (including fewer stacking baskets), it's easier to manage the order, and the pens do not clone themselves! Every personal space in our lives can be handled in this way to maintain harmony.

### *Keepsakes*

It is often the most challenging to let go of items that have symbolic or sentimental attachments. Good advice is to curate those items. This helps to choose specific ones that provide more intense feelings of warmth and joy to you and then let go of the other items. Give yourself enough time for this mental processing and follow it up with rewarding yourself. We often hold on to items that we attach to loss, as if it is meant to bring the person back, when in fact it only reminds us of the grief. When we recognize the value of an item for its true worth, we perceive it with a rational mind instead of an emotional one. This eventually affirms our own worth and we are able to maintain the process.

### *Wardrobes*

We get the hoarder wardrobe and we get the frugal wardrobe. Both need care. Jenny likes to buy clothes on a whim and Jim keeps his clothes dating back from the '60s 'bell-bottom' era stacked in the wardrobe, refusing to let them go. Then, we also have the case of teenage Tim, where the wardrobe becomes the hiding spot for every item he normally leaves on the floor until his mother tells him to clean his room. Nobody wants to open that door for fear of being swamped. Dad can never find the right tie because he never leaves them on the tie rack…

Fast fashion has had a devastating effect on society, stemming from retailers who started to produce trendy, affordable clothes of poor quality to meet the demand of hungry consumers at the end of the previous century. Fashion (or style) became something cheap and convenient, and 30 years later, the world is facing the consequences of the annual production of 92 million tons of textile waste. Where will this go?

If we apply a minimalistic restructuring mindset of creative orderliness to this chaos, we win. Keeping items grouped neatly together in identifiable containers that are appealing to the eye, creates harmony and provides tranquility on top of functionality.

### *Children's Rooms*

When it comes to spaces that children mostly occupy, the question is why the space becomes overrun by toys. Is it a lack of better organization or a matter of giving in to the children's continuous whims? Sadly, overconsumption with children often correlates to overcompensation for feeling unworthy as a parent or being an absent parent. Is the guilt aspect prominent in your parenting? Do you feel that you are giving too many gifts and it is never enough for the child? The answer to these questions provides clarity. Gifts are not supposed to replace time and attention, so investigate the root of the issue. Remember that we pass on our energy to the child, so if we feel unworthy or inadequate, it will show in the interaction. Determine if it is legitimate or unfounded and make the necessary adjustments. We often put too much pressure on ourselves as parents.

An effective method is to plan a three-hour family shift for decluttering, invite all the participants, and promise a reward. Take a Saturday morning and make it pleasurable by playing music and having the children's favorite refreshments available. A team effort spent like this brings rewarding memories of its own. When the children lose interest, ask them which of the items they would keep in their own homes one day and wait for the response! This may just set off some dreaming and visualization that can come in very handy on future decluttering dates.

### *Kitchens*

Kitchens can become clutter chaos magnets. Why do we keep tinned food and rice stacked up for the apocalypse? Rather, ask yourself which ones you would actually eat, check expiry dates, and discard all the excess. Spices also have an expiry date and should be managed regularly to prevent them from taking over. Ask yourself if it is useful to buy a rare item that you need for one recipe only. Many boutique suppliers offer fresh herbs and spices for these rare occasions.

Keeping broken utensils is a hard habit to break, but a very necessary one if you take declutter action. The same mindset applies to duplicates—we do not need four pasta spoons! Plastic containers without lids, and pots without handles can become a nightmare if they are not managed. The key to kitchen success and functionality is keeping the cupboards simple and functional. Place small things in trendy baskets so that you never have to look for them. Keep the counter space open and available for baking and creating to your heart's content. Return your kitchen to the room that used to be the heart of the home, the place where the family gathers for love and sharing.

### *Garage Space*

The definition of a garage is a space where vehicles are kept. Sadly, it ends up becoming the storage space for all the excess from other rooms of our houses. The solution is to imagine that your vehicle has a soul and just like you, probably would enjoy a bit of ambiance and harmony where it sleeps.

### *Other People's Stuff in Your Space*

It is not always easy to keep other people out of your space, but it is always easy to keep their stuff out! Their stuff tends to linger longer as well, so the better you manage it from entering your home in the first place, the more tranquil the relationship will remain. Look at the reasons why it is difficult to say "no," and reconsider the value of the relationship in relation to the stuff...

## FAMILY LIFE AND RELATIONSHIPS

Families matter. Relationships matter. Communication matters. Saying *no* matters.

### *Boundaries and Saying No*

Personal boundaries are crucial to healthy relationships, as they reinforce the limits or rules that we would like to maintain. The boundaries we put up to protect ourselves vary across cultures and situations. Individuals also exhibit different kinds of boundaries depending on their personalities and archetypal conditioning. Healthy boundaries mean being able to say "no" while also allowing other people into your life. On the other hand, rigid boundaries may keep other people always at an emotional and/or physical distance, whereas porous boundaries maintain unhealthy, overinvolved interaction.

We also have time, material, physical, sexual, intellectual, and emotional boundaries that we maintain across various settings and with different individuals. Any violation of these boundaries may cause distress and feelings of being overwhelmed. Mental clutter is one of the biggest violators in all these categories. Feeling constantly bombarded by demanding children, ailing parents, nagging partners, invasive friends, and demanding coworkers all contribute to mental exhaustion. When time constraints and digital overload add further pressure to our lives, we end up with a head overflowing with clutter.

This is when we have to implement, manage, and maintain healthy boundaries. And it starts by being able to say "no." The reasons why we need healthy boundaries are to enhance our self-respect, to clearly communicate our needs in any relationship, to set healthy limits within the connection, and to encourage positive interactions which ultimately enhance mental decluttering. The most obvious reasons why we do not maintain our boundaries are based on fears, guilt, safety concerns, and often because we were not taught how to uphold them. Being mindful of this is the first step to correcting unhealthy habits and to implementing new goals.

### *Communicating*

Communication is not only about talking—it also involves listening. Human beings tend to focus on themselves while communicating. We also anticipate and prepare our responses even before the other person finishes their statement. As a result, numerous misunderstandings happen simply because people do not engage in 'two-way street' communication. Many of these escalate to anger, sadness, and various other negative forms of emotional expression.

Apart from the verbal and non-verbal elements (like facial expression, and body language) of communication, it should be clear, honest, and relevant to the topic. Information can easily be misunderstood if we do not follow these basic principles. In addition to this, we should also consider the effect of external influences on communication. Aspects like background noise disturbances, climate challenges, environmental factors, stress and anxiety issues, visual distraction, and unrealistic assumptions made while communicating; also play a role. It is much more conducive to resolve if you have the "clean-up-your-room" conversation with your teenager outside his chaotic nest.

### *Toxic People*

Sometimes other people's presence clutters our mind space to such an extent that we cannot focus. It can be exhausting and downright stressful to manage people on top of everything else. This is why careful consideration of who you spend your valuable time with, how frequently, and how you spend your time with others should be taken. Letting go of the people who do not add value to your life or who break you down, may be challenging, but it is not impossible. Start by limiting interaction with online connections. Sometimes this simply means sharing a coffee in a public space to explain why you prefer reduced contact. Other times, more forceful avoidance may be necessary. Your goal should be to create a more harmonious space for healthy and valuable interaction. The ultimate aim is to be mindful of self-care without inflicting unnecessary harm on others.

## LIFESTYLE, SOCIAL ACTIVITIES

Social activities are important for our well-being. They are supposed to destress us, reduce our anxiety levels, and enhance our lifestyles. Unfortunately, this is not always the case. We tend to overcommit not only to social groups and clubs, but also to family and friends. This influences our hectic schedules and exhausting time frames, simply making us feel overwhelmed and frustrated. We end up spending all our time pleasing others, instead of rejuvenating our souls. Pastimes and hobbies regularly become projects started and never finished. When we reach this point, it is time to sit down and breathe again. It is time to re-evaluate the necessity of our commitments and responsibilities with mindful attention to self-care. And sometimes it is simply a matter of letting go and moving on.

### *Social Media and Technology*

Computers can become clutter nightmares. Modern-day society swamps digital systems with information overload. Even our (too many!) social media pages can become duplicates and useless 'stock' storage that serve no purpose at all. And the real problem is that it can happen overnight! The worst is that we all fear that we may lose what we store on our many digital devices. As a result, we double up on storage space and have cloud one and cloud two, and back-up three and four and five, ad infinitum. When our computer crashes, we immediately get a panic attack (forgetting that we have all these backup memories in place) and become more overwhelmed. The simple solution to all this drama is simplicity and immediacy!

Find a simple system that works well for you, and maintain it daily with the same concept of bins (folders)—the stuff to save, the stuff to attend to urgently, and the stuff that can go. Unsubscribe from emails that are cluttering your inbox, delete unnecessary apps from your smartphone, block advertisements, sync technology, and simplify social media connections and communication. The key to keeping your technical world manageable is to treat it as you tend to your kitchen—daily, orderly, and with purpose.

### *Outsourcing*

Big businesses that have to manage their global markets often turn to outsourcing. The external providers bring benefits like reduced costs and more flexibility when serving customers on an agreed standard. Hence, online buying, call-center operators, online marketing, and AI recognition are 21st century concepts that we are all familiar with. But outsourcing also has its disadvantages. We often lose our quietude when we allow social media platforms, call-center operators, and internet sources to shift our direction and steal our focus through advertising, online marketing, and endless scrolling. The media is rife with sources that control our choices in this way. If we do not manage the bombardment that directs our thoughts, we lose our logical reasoning. The best solution against mindless online collaboration is to make these platforms (and companies) work for us, and not the other way around. It's time to become mindful of the value of outsourcing...

# 7

# TIME AND SPACE

Our schedules can be just as cluttered as anything else, and this often leads to knock-on clutter in our lives. Let's take back our time and take back our lives. Let's start giving instead of taking. Let's connect with people instead of things. Ultimately, we have to reassess our goals in life and take control. We frantically start and stop and leave the 'less important' things incomplete in an endless cycle that feeds itself. Managing time infuses space management.

## A CONCEPT OF TIME

Modern-day lifestyles and hectic schedules quickly fill up our lives and make us forget what time truly is. Sometimes we have to remind ourselves of our root beliefs about time and its relativity. Time and space are linked and co-exist inseparably. Time creates space and space creates time! Steven Covey reminds us to pay careful attention to the difference between importance and urgency in order to manage our time better. He describes urgency as the "weight" of a task and importance as the time it's "due." He further establishes four quadrants of time management, namely:

1. Important and urgent – these are crises, immediately due tasks, or things that we cannot stop thinking about.
2. Important and not urgent – these are generally long-term projects.
3. Not important and urgent – these are social invitations or distractions.
4. Not important and not urgent – these are things like aimless social media scrolling, internet browsing, online shopping, and generally procrastinating activities.

Keeping our awareness fixed on these time management concepts is helpful to make time more valuable and more efficient in our daily lives.

## TIME IS OUR MOST VALUABLE ASSET

Time remains our most valuable asset. It also remains fleeting. We can never get it back. The time to become aware of its value in our existence has come! When we are mindful of and grateful for every present moment, we are fully engaged with time and enjoying its benefits. How many of us have regrets of times when we were not fully present that we can never return to? It is thus useful to learn to prioritize the things that truly matter, focus on urgent matters, and engage with careful attention to these matters in order to wholeheartedly enjoy time efficiently.

## THE BEAUTY OF SCHEDULES AND ROUTINES

We constantly have to make decisions, and every decision-making opportunity creates stress. If we can tone these decisions down to a regular rhythm, then we manage the amount of stress they produce. Routines are helpful here. When we do not have to make additional decisions about things that can become daily routines and habits, we give our brains a rest. In this way, we leave our decision-making energy for the important things!

Better sleep patterns, starting your day well, and making time for enjoyable moments with loved ones all contribute to more healthy lifestyles. A helpful habit is to keep routines at scheduled times in your daily planner. Alan Lakein's list of the ABC method is an effective reminder to prioritize. He encourages making lists and naming the items "must do," "should do," and "nice to do," to establish their chronological importance in your daily routine. It is also important to stay realistic and fluid, especially with a work-life schedule that you have to balance with home and family responsibilities.

Taking a break occasionally should be part of our scheduled routines. Regular vacations, weekend trips away, daily bicycle rides or walks, or simply abstaining from constantly checking work emails and answering phone calls can silence the chatter and help to unwind and recover energy again.

## PLANNING AND PRIORITIZING OUR LIVES

Planning our days should pivot around what is important to us. In doing so, we are able to let go of what is not important. The act of simplifying our lives is not a complex issue, it is simply about how immune we have become to complexity (or multiplicity). The basic principles that guide us back to essential simplicity are asking "Is this necessary?" and being able to answer—without hesitation—"no." Keeping our eyes on what is essential will maintain our focus on what matters. How many times are we being pulled to yet another social interaction while our gut feeling tells us "No, it is not really necessary to go"?

If you still hesitate to say “no” to your question, then ask yourself if it aligns with your purpose and long-term vision. Only through gaining this kind of clarity and priority to staying focused, do we regain the power of always having a choice. This power is the extremely liberating balancing act of decluttering. Learn to draw the line, say “no” to things that do not serve you, eliminate events that do not contribute to your well-being, and limit interaction with people who clutter your space. If you do not have clarity about your values, you will not be able to draw the line and say “no.” Our intention must be focused and simplified to ultimately lead to a fulfilled life.

## BALANCING TIME

Time management is crucial to a balanced life. Avoid wasting energy on senseless complaining and mindless activities that only steal time. Be attentive to abusing the habit of busyness or simply passing time mindlessly. Schedule valuable time more effectively and remember to also set aside some time for simply being. Take control and find harmony. The value of time lies in the balancing of the scales. Balancing our time well means prioritizing the interactions and spaces where we spend most of our time. These include family, work, and ourselves.

### *Family*

There lies a fine balance between family time and work time, along with how we prioritize them. Some people believe that work should take priority and others believe that family comes first. Other individuals say they work for their family and some say that healthy familial relationships encourage and enhance work quality. However we look at it, the value allocated to family time should not be underestimated. There are endless sayings about the value of family time over success, and that time spent with your family can never be measured in financial terms. A simple act like laughing together can bring an overwhelmed family together again. Mother Teresa said "Smile at each other. Make time for each other in your family" (*29 Family Time Quotes - Inspirational Words of Wisdom*, n.d.). Nobody has ever uttered the words that spending time with their children was a waste or regret of their time. It's about finding a mindful balance in every present moment.

### *Work*

Work will never disappear. This is why it is so important to enjoy your job so that schedules, deadlines, demands, and responsibilities don't feel like a dreadful prison. Our aim should be to avoid burnout. It is useful to apply not only physical distancing to our work at times, but also mental distancing by shutting our minds down from work responsibilities. Maintain boundaries and work hours and manage related interactions with colleagues for healthy well-being. Avoid wasting time by checking and rechecking to-do lists. Instead, tackle the list from top to bottom, complete it, or let it go. The importance of flexibility should also be on our lists! Balance life and work commitments in order to generate a healthy lifestyle.

### *Me-Time*

Me, myself, and I are as important as having compassion for others and sharing with them. But sometimes we have to put ourselves first in order to be helpful to others. We cannot deplete ourselves and expect to stay healthy. We nurture ourselves in order to care for others. Artist, writer, and Stanford professor Jenny Odell has an alternative approach to what she calls "interiority." In an interview with *The Guardian*, she mentions:

I think interiority is really underrated right now. That could just be my own bias. I seem to spend a lot of time trying to figure out ways to get away from people. [Laughs] I think that there is a lot to be said for being alone with your thoughts for an extended period of time (Shechet, 2019).

Odell places importance on the effect of being in nature and noticing things outside of ourselves to become more aware of our internal thoughts. She claims that a redirection toward the natural habitat is a "strategy for resisting a profit-driven tech landscape that, in separating our bodies and co-opting our attention, is possibly torching our ability to live meaningful lives, and prevent us from noticing." I would add that apart from this valuable reminder to connect our inner beings to nature and be more observant, we should also stay focused on our goals. To do this, we simply have to structure our days and stick to the planning.

## HOW TO DO NOTHING LIKE A MASTER

*Il dolce far niente* is the Italian phrase for doing sweet nothing. Many cultures have similar powerful phrases that evoke the tranquility of the art of doing nothing, but I can visualize the powerful image of a person sitting under the Italian skies during a humid summer and keeping quite still to avoid the heat. Watching life pass by. Doing *niente*. Simply being. I cannot imagine anything more rejuvenating to a weary soul.

Why do we have the constant need to always *do* something? Why can't we just sometimes *be*? We keep cluttering our lives with endless lists of self-imposed pressure producing more pressure to be more productive as we go along, and we end up feeling drained from it all. We convince ourselves that we have to be doing something 'worthwhile' all the time. We obsess about a 'busyness' that we believe will ensure success. We make it even worse by feeling guilty or anxious if we are not actively doing something. We fail to pause, reflect, and look inwardly, only to end up feeling overworked, over-engaged, overwhelmed, exhausted, anxious, and developing stress-related diseases.

*Il dolce far niente* is certainly not a synonym for laziness, but instead, it promotes the power and pleasure of being idle with the sole purpose of finding relaxation. Only in this space is the mind truly free and liberated from cognitive demands. The mind can leisurely float in the space of nothingness, wind down, and recharge. We need to engage in this activity on a regular basis—we owe it to our times. Sometimes we have to procrastinate mindfully and daydream to restore the senses. Even researchers have found the problem-solving benefits of daydreaming, concluding that moments of idleness make us more creative. If some misinterpretation from our conditioned past memories evoke too many feelings of guilt when we apply idleness, they should be addressed and amended to suit a more simplistic and healthy lifestyle. Committing to a less cluttered life can become a priority if you set your mind to it, take a breath, and start the process, slowly and mindfully.

# 8

# WHAT IF IT HAPPENS AGAIN?

You might worry that you will relapse into your old ways, or maybe you have decluttered before and it didn't 'stick.' How do we wrestle with this? Iain Thomas sums it up correctly:

And every day, the world will drag you by the hand, yelling, 'This is important! And this is important! And this is important! You need to worry about this! And this! And this!' And each day, it's up to you to yank your hand back, put it on your heart and say 'No. This is what's important' (Marthaler, n.d.).

## TWEAK YOUR HABITS

It's so easy to fall back on old habits when we relax in our homes, until we unexpectedly realize that our minds feel cluttered and we are stressed or irritable. When these spaces become cluttered again, we should analyze what went wrong. Try to think of inventive ways to prevent it from happening again—the solution to clutter problems is often very clear. Prioritize the important and urgent things again. Reassess your to-do and not-to-do lists and complete them. Get up earlier, make the bed, have less coffee during the day, skip that extra snack or extra glass of wine, make a deliberate attempt at placing things where they belong, start your day by doing the thing you hate the most first, change your diet—do whatever it takes to tweak your unique clutter habits back to simplicity again. You've done it once, you can do it again!

## ONE THING AT A TIME

Start with your clothes: Try to minimize the essentials into a smaller space and donate the rest. You probably only wear the same few pieces all the time. From there, tackle the kitchen cupboards and be very specific about the functionality of your appliances. Chuck the many duplicates and items that you hardly ever use. Recycle and donate what you don't use too. Throw away the things that are damaged and cannot be fixed. Follow the same process with books, magazines, and extra paper clutter. After these few steps, you should be back to your newfound minimalist habits!

## RELY ON ROUTINES AND ASK FOR HELP

Good habits and regular routines are like gold dust. Give them attention and maintain them well. If your routine doesn't encourage a simple uncluttered life, change the routine. Stick to schedules and keep to your planning. Reinvent these if they have become obsolete. Do you run out of the house every morning with a bagel and coffee on-the-go, a crumpled coat, and shoelaces still untied as you rush to work? Are you too busy to sit still? Then, it's time to delegate or ask for help. Simplicity implies how to know if and when you need it. Organize that packing party again and maintain your buddy system for support.

## STAY MINDFUL OF YOUR CLUTTER HABITS

It is important to have a clear idea of the reasons why you declutter. Are they based on environmental awareness—are you thinking of the carbon footprint that you leave behind? Are budget limitations forcing you to declutter and simplify your environment and lifestyle? Or do you have a travel plan in place with related implications and requirements? Ask yourself these questions to maintain your focus. Determine what you believe in and what you stand for, in order to hold course and come back after a momentary relapse. In addition to these concepts, always stay attentive to the clutter habits that brought you here in the first place. When you have worked through them and identified their roots and causes, stay mindful of the triggers and manage them to avoid clutter from taking your life over again.

## VISUALIZE

We often achieve success easier when we think with our 'eyes.' People interpret the world visually. Look at the before and after photos of the rooms again to re-establish your visualization and goals. Always bear your goals in mind, and imagine the new uncluttered life you want. Anticipate the new you that you frequently dream of. Visualize that empty computer desktop and "eat the frog first" as they say, while keeping the image of what you will gain afterward in mind.

## AFFIRMATIONS FOR SIMPLICITY

Keep assuring yourself that simplicity is the key to your harmony. Invent new affirmations occasionally to motivate yourself to achieve your goals. Keep reminding yourself of your goals. Create simplicity on all levels of your life. Your internal serenity flows over to the external areas of your life. Find that inner harmony again and allow it to guide you back to simplicity. It has been said that Gandhi achieved much more than most people, and he always appeared to be relaxed. There is value in calmness. Tranquility generates productivity!

## OBSERVE AND REFRAME

Unhelpful thoughts and beliefs should be re-evaluated constantly. Always be aware of the incredible progress already made. Remember that minimalism is a process and lifestyle that implies one step forward and one step back sometimes. Relapsing is acceptable because it's possible to fix it again. After all, we are all only human, and living implies momentary lapses of weakness. After a relapse, know that if you still have the *intention* of being minimalistic, a relapse is not the end of the world! It doesn't mean that you are going back to a consumeristic life again. Simply re-establish your intentions again in line with your goals and see it as a normal part of life.

## DON'T GIVE UP

Clutter accumulates with negative feelings. It is a method of distraction. So, ask yourself why the clutter happened again, identify the reasons behind the relapse and your clutter habit, and determine what needs are not being met and what you can learn from this. Our feelings speak, so listen to them. Find the underlying weakness and learn from that to improve. If you can identify the weakness behind your clutter habit, you will be able to avoid temptations and triggers. Make a pros-and-cons list to keep you focused on the goal and place it somewhere visible where it often catches your eye. Remember that falling back one step doesn't mean paradise is lost.

## SELF-COMPASSION

Let's stop and think about the concept of compassion. We all know what it means, but how often do we remind ourselves of its value in our lives? Having compassion means being able to turn toward suffering, and having self-compassion implies turning gently toward your own suffering. I think that many of us fail in this regard. Compassion is an important part of communication (and vice versa) and self-compassion fights demeaning self-talk. If you ask yourself what your best friend would say to you if you made a mistake, how differently would you respond to your faults? The guiding line is to instead listen to your friend's response and not to your own overly critical inner voice. A common example of the heartless criticism of our inner voice is when we lose our keys—a friend's response would be much more compassionate and solution-driven.

Be grateful by noticing what is available at every moment. The story of the toilet paper syndrome (we only value the toilet paper when it's not there!) is useful to remind us of being more mindful and compassionate with ourselves. Have some patience and kindness with yourself, not only with others. Make that mindset shift, and don't always label yourself as being bad or a failure when it is only a temporary relapse.

## DECLUTTERING DON'TS

The following things should be avoided in the decluttering process. Also, keep mindful attention to relapsing to them!

- One Thing at a Time – don't take on too much all at once. Tackle one task daily. Only focus on one decluttering project, and don't start another before completion. Declutter one room daily. Minimize one social issue before you attempt the next. Cut down digital projects into bite-sized, achievable chunks.

- Don't Rush It – remember that a focused approach with a tranquil mind is much more productive than anything rushed. When we rush, we shove things into corners. When we think, we place them where they belong.
- Don't Feel Bad – have patience with yourself. You are human and are allowed to struggle. Nobody likes to clean a mess, especially not an emotional one!
- Reward Yourself – never minimalize your gains or how much you have improved over time. Celebrate the wins and always reward yourself after accomplishing a major task. Remind yourself constantly of your previous successes.
- Buddy System – don't be alone, create a network of supporters, and don't feel bad to depend on them sometimes.
- Don't Forget – never forget to stay mindful. After reading this book, you will have all the tools to help you maintain a mindful approach. Golden words for decluttering are concentration, focus, commitment, intention, routines, balance, and simplicity. Never forget them.
- Intention – Don't just declutter to declutter, try to declutter mindfully, and always with intention.
- The Joneses – don't worry about what other people are doing. Find your own way of doing things that work for you.
- Justification – don't try to justify your stuff. Don't bluff yourself. Be truthful to yourself. Justify your goal instead.

# 9

# THE BEAUTY OF A SIMPLE LIFE

*The beauty of a simple life is born from how little I choose to get along with and not how much. –Itani*

Minimalism is the art of simplifying and organizing what we see. For a minimalist, the importance is that everything serves a specific purpose, has a meaning, and adds value. The value is directed at material things in our lives, as well as the art of living in the world. The beauty of applying a minimalist outlook to create more ease, flow, and peace in our daily lives is a reality to embrace with open arms!

## THE ART OF SIMPLICITY

What is minimalism? It is more than not having things, it is also a mindful lifestyle that intentionally influences the actions that you take. Commitment to minimalism is important to the process of becoming a minimalist. Take certain steps consistently and commit to your decisions and their resulting changes. A minimalistic outlook means showing up and doing the work, even if it's tricky or not perfect, instead of giving up. You can always ask for help if needed.

Simplifying your lifestyle and habits also means giving attention to the valuable skill of prioritizing. First, define the relevant values and principles to understand what is important to you. Don't let life define them for you, but rather, make the choice to define them yourself. Give priority to the things that matter the most and let the others go. If family is everything to you, then focus on family matters when you simplify. Scrutinize your life on a daily basis and make it a habit to do this naturally, like brushing your teeth. Focus mostly on items that you haven't used, determine their value to your life, reflect, and re-assess your possessions while you scrutinize your life into simplicity.

Foster the ability to tidy up, and schedule this daily. Things get out of hand very quickly if you do not follow a system of maintaining order. Find what works well for you and stick to it while encouraging other members of the household to support you in this endeavor. Take small but regular actions based on who you are and what works for you and your cohabitants. If you properly care for things, you have less to repair and get rid of, and they do not need to be replaced. This is why general maintenance is crucial to a simplified lifestyle. When items do need fixing, determine if it is really necessary to fix them and re-assess the value of having them replaced before you jump into getting more stuff. Sharing appliances or co-ownership (like lawnmowers, library books, public transport, vacuum cleaners) means pairing down the number of items in your household with fewer items and less maintenance. After all, the aim is to reduce in your life!

We have looked at how we subconsciously and easily attach to things and memories on an emotional level. Shouldn't we actually emotionally attach to people instead of to things? An item should not replace a person—in fact, it cannot replace a person. These emotional attachments create clutter on all levels, and we draw them into our habits subconsciously. Creating mindful attention to this faulty habit will improve simplicity.

## CREATE EASE, FAST

There are a few foolproof ways to tackle a cluttered life and prevent it from taking over.

### *Get Into the Water*

Some of us do not like to swim, but sometimes swimming is the only way to cross the river. Keeping a mindset of temporary discomfort to find long-term harmony makes this swimming bearable. If the clutter in your room, on your desk, in your cupboards, in your social interactions, on online portals and your mailbox, in relationships, and in your head feels like a vast river with infested crocodiles—get in, and swim to a better shore.

### *Use Positive Affirmations*

Affirmations are effective de-stressors to calm down a racing mind. I love to keep one at hand for every challenging situation. "Create more, consume less" (Itani, 2021a) or words like "Let it be easy," and "Everyday things are working out" have brought immense calm in the midst of storms and chaos. We have to remind ourselves constantly of these affirmations—"I am enough," "I have enough," and "I am going to be okay." Find your personal inspirational words that work for you in any situation and repeat them until balance returns. There are numerous meditation affirmations available online to set you off. Sometimes a sentence of hope from a child's innocent perspective also helps. My younger daughter once told me "at least you are not a penguin that has to run." Now, I 'affirm' every challenging situation out of *penguinhood*—"I am not a penguin, I am not a penguin, I am not a penguin!"

### *Meditate*

Meditation is one of the most efficient ways to combat stress and anxiety. It wards off depression while you combat emotional burdens. Researchers at Harvard have found that a simple meditation routine can rebuild the gray matter in the brain within eight weeks and thus restore physiological benefits to the body. The gray matter of the brain is responsible for our cognitive processes which include perception and primary thinking that assists with processing information (Riopel, 2019a). Apart from meditation's cognitive benefits, it also helps with reducing blood pressure, relieving anxiety, and pain management.

Mindfulness meditation stabilizes the present moment by avoiding distractions about the past or future that tend to clutter the mind. You focus on the moment and what it has to offer without judgment or overthinking. This could be done while you are engaged in something creatively, washing dishes, or enjoying a shower—the key is to pay focused attention to the activity. Mindful walking meditations are similar in nature. It is a highly healing form of meditation, especially when practiced in nature when you engage with your senses. Sensing the breeze on your skin, hearing the sound of the soil under your feet, and smelling the scent of pine needles enhance tranquility.

Allowing emotions to surface during focused meditations on an object is creative and intense while improving concentration and satisfactory results. Progressive muscle meditation is a healing technique that involves focused contracting and releasing of muscles, starting from your head and moving progressively down to your feet, or vice versa.

A mere visualization session (like daydreaming) can be similarly beneficial. You may even visualize the things that you want to implement in your uncluttered home, imagining the improved appearance of the rooms or cupboard spaces. Visual 'decluttering' like this is a necessary step to visualize your goals and aims. Imagine sitting inside that uncluttered space and experiencing how it makes you feel, to kickstart your planning. If your intention is to declutter your mind, visualize a walk along the beach or in a lush forest and experience the sensation.

### *Reframing Go-to Phrase*

Here are some useful phrases to utilize in extreme scenarios:

- In this moment, I am okay.
- Go slow, dear mind.
- Do less, choose one.
- Remember to breathe!
- Concentrate.
- Keep focusing.

Try to find phrases that you remember almost instinctively and keep asking yourself if something is really beneficial to your life—find the value of its necessity and make the adjustments.

### *Get Outside or Exercise*

Ground yourself in nature's serenity when you feel overwhelmed. Stretch in the sun, take a walk in a forest, or sit on the beach and look at the sunset. Keep your body active with regular exercise and start moving again. Do not let that gym membership go to waste and prevent the dumbell doorstops from becoming dusty. It only takes a little motivation to step outside and go. Most of the time, you come back revived and rejuvenated, and your whole life feels manageable and calm again.

### *Journal*

There are a million benefits to journaling, but the most powerful ones have definite long-term value. It reduces stress, helps maintain focus by keeping your memory active, enhances mood that contributes to your well-being, benefits your emotional health by regulating emotions, and also strengthens your immune system. Apart from these benefits, taking the time to read through your past journals provide a multitude of coping skills and insight to understanding yourself better. It also provides some reflective humor at times!

### *Breathe*

Breathing is always a sure way to tranquility. Sometimes we actually forget to breathe altogether! It has been found that the most effective breathing rhythms are belly breathing, and mindful meditative breathing. Thích Nhât Hạnh describes his meditation tactics as "Breathing in I know I am breathing in. Breathing out I know I am breathing out" (Schwartz & Pinterest, n.d.). Always straighten your back and relax your shoulders while breathing.

#### Bellows Breath

This breathing method boosts energy and leaves you feeling invigorated. Start with a 15-second session and slowly increase. While sitting, inhale and exhale rapidly through the nose, keeping the mouth closed and relaxed. It is a fast and noisy exercise, and the in-and-out breaths must be equally long and as short as possible, while the diaphragm moves quickly.

### 4-7-8 Relaxing Breathing

Inhale for four counts, hold for seven counts, exhale for eight counts. This exercise is a natural nervous system tranquilizer and stress preventative breathing method, and may cause feelings of lightheadedness when doing it the first time. Let the tip of your tongue touch the roof of your mouth, behind the upper front teeth. Keep it in place, and count to four while inhaling through your nose. Hold your breath and exhale through the mouth while counting the rhythm of four-seven-eight.

### Counting Breath

Try to maintain this exercise for ten minutes. It's relaxing and soothing. Take deep breaths naturally in and out. Mentally count to one as you inhale, and slowly exhale while you count to two. Continue the same rhythm while increasing the counts to three, and so forth. Repeat the cycles and count for as long as you feel comfortable.

### Abdominal Breathing

Lie on your back on a supportive surface with your head on a pillow. Bend your knees or drape them over a pillow. Place one hand on your rib cage, with the other on your chest, and take a deep breath until you feel your stomach rise. Tighten stomach muscles and exhale through your lips. Do this five to ten minutes daily.

### *Ease Into Gratitude*

Meditating on gratitude has been proven as being highly beneficial and associated with feelings of increased happiness and reduced stress. Taking a short moment to stop and acknowledge gratitude is all it takes. A simple method is to close your eyes and reflect on an item that brings joy or something that you notice in your immediate environment. It can also be a reflection on someone who has made an impact on your life, even a stranger who made a difference in your day. It can be the first cup of warm soothing coffee after a restless night. Just focus on being grateful for the small token in that particular moment and this will extend feelings of gratitude to other areas of your life.

Our lives are made up of polarities. We only experience the concept of light when we understand the concept of darkness, or joy versus its opposing force—suffering. Taking time to remind ourselves of this—and appreciating both—is a soothing and calming exercise. It helps to bring gratitude for the things that we have. It may sound like a negative activity, but sometimes the mere thought of losing someone and imagining the resultant emotions is an excellent gratitude practice and allows for a mindful reflection of what the present moment has to offer. It helps us to count our blessings when we feel overwhelmed. Replace mental clutter and mindless chatter with ease and gratitude.

### *Nap and Snack*

At times our sleeping patterns get severely disrupted by emotional disturbances, stress, and feelings of hopelessness. Instead of buying or accumulating more stuff, and instead of wasting aimless scrolling time online—take a short nap. Even if it is the most difficult thing to do, getting up early makes a huge difference to your day. You can start this process with a healthy snack if it is difficult to get out of bed. Coffee also helps! The truth is that longer days have more health benefits, and researchers have found that early risers show better organizational skills and higher productivity levels in general. Another useful technique (if you cannot take a nap) is to make time to just sit. Simply sitting and calming your thoughts can restore tranquility.

If you focus your energy on maintaining a simplified lifestyle, you also transmit your serenity to the people around you. Every time when you complete a task with deliberate concentration, you enhance your self-worth and awareness.

# CONCLUSION

*Chaos in the world brings uneasiness, but it also allows the opportunity for creativity and growth. –Tom Barrett*

How do we know when we have enough? What *is* enough? What can we choose to be 'enough' in our lives? This book gave you the tools to tackle the mess. We looked at the most important aspects of removing clutter from your life, which were as follows:

- We analyzed the stigma of clutter and its personality identities.
- We addressed the consequences of complexity and chaos.
- We looked at the causes of cluttering on various life dimensions.
- We scrutinized the details of mental decluttering.
- We tried to understand and interpret emotional clutter.
- We faced physical decluttering and found ways to restructure our lives.

- We examined the concepts of time and space and the resultant importance in planning.
- We considered the decluttering don'ts and how to prevent relapsing.
- We learned to value the art of simplicity and know how to find its beauty.

## ENCOURAGEMENT

There are wise words out there that say if we feel a little grumpy, we should go and be kind. Do something for someone. That someone may even be you. That someone may be your home space, the space you share with significant others, or simply your mental space. In your past, you probably felt that you did not have enough, or maybe that you were not enough, and you used to fill the gaps in your life with 'stuff' and 'busyness.' There is no shame in this. There is no reason to feel guilty. You are beautiful because you are human.

In *The Life-Changing Magic of Tidying Up*, Marie Kondo writes:

> The process of assessing how you feel about the things you own, identifying those that have fulfilled their purpose, expressing your gratitude, and bidding them farewell, is really about examining your inner self, a rite of passage to a new life (2021).

This process of shedding and assessing also applies to digital, mental, and relational clutter. Shedding those memories and toxic connections opens up a space of simplified freedom. Tranquility flows from this and harmony is restored.

Congratulations! You have found simplicity in the chaos. You have improved your mindset. Now you have the knowledge and ability to identify your physical and mental clutter, and you can understand how the mess found you! From this moment forward, it's in your hands to recognize your unique struggles and establish solutions to them. I hope this book has given you the motivation to empower yourself toward success and serenity.

*If you have found this book useful, do share the delightful and inspirational moments with others. I would be delighted if you leave a sincere review that could encourage others who also want to enhance their lives like you did.*

# REFERENCES

3 Ways to Prioritize. (2019, October 30). *3 ways to prioritize*. Academic Success Center. https://success.oregonstate.edu/learning/prioritize

*29 family time quotes - inspirational words of wisdom*. (n.d.). Www.wow4u.com. https://www.wow4u.com/familyquotes5/

*A quote by C.G. Jung*. (2022). Www.goodreads.com. https://www.goodreads.com/quotes/22585-in-all-chaos-there-is-a-cosmos-in-all-disorder

Admin. (2021, October 17). *Tom Barrett - Chaos in the world brings uneasiness, but it also allows the opportunity for creativity and growth.* Motivational Quotes - Daily Quotes for Instagram 2021. https://www.cactusquotes.com/affirmations-for-opportunities/tom-barrett-chaos-in-the-world-brings-uneasiness-but-it-also-allows-the-opportunity-for-creativity-and-growth/

APDO. (2021, March 23). *Making clutter count: Decluttering during the pandemic | APDO*. APDO. https://www.apdo.co.uk/blog-decluttering-pandemic/

Bailey, K. (2018, July 31). *5 powerful health benefits of journaling*. Intermountainhealthcare.org. https://intermountainhealthcare.org/blogs/topics/live-well/2018/07/5-powerful-health-benefits-of-journaling/

Becker, J. (2019, October 22). *10 creative ways to declutter your home*. Www.becomingminimalist.com. https://www.becomingminimalist.com/creative-ways-to-declutter/

Becker, J. (2021). *The statistics of clutter*. Www.becomingminimalist.com. https://www.becomingminimalist.com/the-statistics-of-clutter/

Berwager Schreier, A. (2019, March 20). *Your clutter isn't always because you're "messy" — here are 9 causes of the chaos*. Romper. https://www.romper.com/p/9-surprising-causes-of-clutter-according-to-experts-16959986

Big Self School. (2022). *3 reasons your inner critic doesn't want to leave your mind.* Www.bigselfschool.com. https://www.bigselfschool.com/post/3-reasons-your-inner-critic-persists

*boundaries - hoarding*. (2019). Reddit. https://www.reddit.com/r/hoarding/wiki/boundaries

breathe. (2008, March 19). *12 essential rules to live more like a zen monk*. Zen Habits. https://zenhabits.net/12-essential-rules-to-live-more-like-a-zen-monk/

The Canada Life. (2009). *WSMH*. WSMH. https://www.workplacestrategiesformentalhealth.com/resources/the-functions-of-emotions

Cherry, K. (2020a, January 15). *Extrinsic vs. intrinsic motivation: what's the difference?* Verywell Mind. https://www.verywellmind.com/differences-between-extrinsic-and-intrinsic-motivation-2795384

Cherry, K. (2020b, May 17). *The purpose of emotions*. Verywell Mind; Verywellmind. https://www.verywellmind.com/the-purpose-of-emotions-2795181

Cherry, K. (2020c, May 30). *The psychology behind why we wait until the last minute to do things*. Verywell Mind. https://www.verywellmind.com/the-psychology-of-procrastination-2795944

Cherry, K. (2021, February 20). *The big five personality traits*. Verywell Mind. https://www.verywellmind.com/the-big-five-personality-dimensions-2795422

Chrissy. (2021, March 23). *16 surprising clutter statistics that will totally shock you.* Organise My House. https://organisemyhouse.com/clutter-statistics/

Danielle, M. (2017, November 15). *A must-read for overcoming limiting beliefs around clutter*. Miadanielle.com. https://miadanielle.com/destroy-limiting-beliefs-around-clutter/

daraddicted. (2014, March 19). *Outsourcing: Is it good or bad?* Www.youtube.com. https://youtu.be/7qeehDLYa8g

Decluttering, M., Organizing, & LLC. (2017, January 24). *Handling clutter from trauma or loss*. Mindful Decluttering & Organizing. https://clutterfreenow.com/blog/decluttering/handling-clutter-from-trauma-or-loss/

Delagran, L. (2016). *How to deal with fear and anxiety* (S. Towey, Ed.). Taking Charge of Your Health & Wellbeing. https://www.takingcharge.csh.umn.edu/how-deal-fear-and-anxiety

Deschenne, L. (2010, April 16). *20 ways to let go of regrets*. Tiny Buddha. https://tinybuddha.com/blog/20-ways-to-let-go-of-regrets/

DOWell. (2020, November 16). *HINT: Your clutter is caused by your trauma*. Www.youtube.com. https://youtu.be/e61FaKJL3pc

Economy, P. (2015, November 5). *26 brilliant quotes on the super power of words*. Inc.com; Inc. https://www.inc.com/peter-economy/26-brilliant-quotes-on-the-super-power-of-words.html

Einzelgänger. (2021, July 29). *What will we truly miss? (The fear of missing out)*. Www.youtubc.com. https://youtu.be/6jX9ANAgVuY

Elizabeth Scott. (2019). *What are the main causes of stress?* Verywell Mind. https://www.verywellmind.com/what-are-the-main-causes-of-stress-3145063

Ellis, S. (2020, January 7). *What emotional numbness really feels like* (T. J. Legg, Ed.). Greatist. https://greatist.com/health/emotional-numbness#prevention

Engle, J. (2020, March 11). *Stress, worry and anxiety are all different. How do you cope with each?* The New York Times. https://www.nytimes.-com/2020/03/11/learning/stress-worry-and-anxiety-are-all-different-how-do-you-cope-with-each.html?action=click&pgtype=Article&state=default&module=styln-mental-health&variant=show®ion=BELOW_MAIN_CONTENT&block=storyline_flex_guide_recirc

Fallon, A. (2015, December 14). *Getting over the fear of not enough*. Allison Fallon. https://allisonfallon.com/not-enough/

Fulton, B. (2020, October 27). *The benefits of gratitude and how to get started* (J. Johnson, Ed.). Healthline. https://www.healthline.com/health/benefits-of-gratitude-practice#benefits

Goldberg, S. (2016). *The 10 rules of change*. Psychology Today. https://www.psychologytoday.com/us/articles/200209/the-10-rules-change

Good Therapy. (2015). *Therapy for control issues*. Goodtherapy.org. https://www.goodtherapy.org/learn-about-therapy/issues/control-issues

Goodreads. (2022). *A quote by Iain S. Thomas*. Www.goodreads.com. https://www.goodreads.com/quotes/997789-and-every-day-the-world-will-drag-you-by-the

Happy and Authentic. (2021, November 21). *How to deal with a clutter relapse as a minimalist*. Www.youtube.com. https://youtu.be/L5bRc01oEcE

Happy and Authentic. (2022, June 19). *Minimalism 101 | How should a true minimalist act?* Www.youtube.com. https://youtu.be/CLCJFpUrq0M

Health, P. B. (2011, August 11). *Clutter addiction*. Promises Behavioral Health. https://www.promises.com/addiction-blog/clutter-addiction/

Hone, J. (2017, January 23). *Psychologists reveal what your household clutter says about your state of mind*. Domain; Domain. https://www.domain.com.au/news/psychologists-reveal-what-your-household-clutter-says-about-your-state-of-mind-20170120-gttusa/

*How to create healthy boundaries*. (n.d.). https://www.uky.edu/hr/sites/www.uky.edu.hr/files/wellness/images/Conf14_Boundaries.pdf

Ishler, J. (2021, September 16). *Are you carrying "emotional baggage" here's how to break free* (J. Litner, Ed.). Healthline. https://www.healthline.com/health/mind-body/how-to-release-emotional-baggage-and-the-tension-that-goes-with-it#How-do-emotions-get-trapped?

ISMA. (n.d.). *How to identify stress | ISMA Stress Management Association*. Isma.org.uk. https://isma.org.uk/how-to-identify-stress

Itani, O. (2021a, January 28). *Create more than you consume if you want to worry less and feel more fulfilled*. OMAR ITANI. https://www.omaritani.com/blog/create-more-consume-less

Itani, O. (2021b, July 23). *How simplifying your life helps you find inner peace and harmony*. OMAR ITANI. https://www.omaritani.com/blog/peace-and-simplicity-vs-multiplicity

Johnson, C. (2018, October 16). *The 7 steps to living a zen lifestyle*. Blys. https://getblys.com.au/7-steps-zen-massage-zen-lifestyle/

Kondo, M. (Director). (n.d.). *Sparking joy with Marie Kondo* [Netflix].

Le Beau Lucchesi, E. (2019, January 3). *The unbearable heaviness of clutter.* The New York Times. https://www.nytimes.com/2019/01/03/well/mind/clutter-stress-procrastination-psychology.html

Marelisa. (2018, June 3). *10 ways to make your day more zen: How to have a zen-like day -*. Daringtolivefully.com. https://daringtolivefully.com/make-your-day-more-zen

Marthaler, S. (n.d.). *3 things to do when you've had a clutter relapse - BLOG | Sandy Marthaler*. Https://Www.sandymarthaler.com/. https://www.sandymarthaler.com/3-things-to-do-when-youve-had-a-clutter-relapse/?utm_source=rss&utm_medium=rss&utm_campaign=3-things-to-do-when-youve-had-a-clutter-relapse

Maté, Dr. G. (2022, March 19). *How your past trauma really works | Dr Gabor Maté*. Www.youtube.com. https://youtu.be/UI6C3ahHpnc

Matthew, J. (Director). (2021). *The minimalists: Less is now* [Netflix].

Mayo Clinic. (2018). *Anxiety disorders - symptoms and causes*. Mayo Clinic; Mayo Foundation for Medical Education and Research. https://www.mayoclinic.org/diseases-conditions/anxiety/symptoms-causes/syc-20350961

Melody. (2021, August 26). *4 ways to channel your emotional energy at work*. Melody Wilding. https://melodywilding.com/4-ways-to-channel-your-emotional-energy-at-work/

Miedaner, T. (2019, October 31). *How to break through scarcity thinking and overwhelm: Two more clutter archetypes*. LifeCoach.com. https://www.lifecoach.com/articles/simplify-clutter/how-to-break-through-scarcity-thinking-and-over whelm-two-more-clutter-archetypes/

*Minimalism ❖ Declutter with Marie Kondo ❖ 30 tips to design your life*. (2021, November 16). Www.youtube.com. https://youtu.be/ZBofvLQdmZ8

Morin, A. (n.d.). *The Verywell Mind podcast with editor-in-chief Amy Morin*. Verywell Mind. https://www.verywellmind.com/the-verywell-mind-podcast-5113058

Morin, A. (2018). *5 ways to simplify your life*. Psychology Today. https://www.psychologytoday.com/us/blog/what-mentally-strong-people-dont-do/201807/5-ways-simplify-your-life

Morin, A. (2022). *The Verywell Mind podcast with Amy Morin on Apple Podcasts*. Apple Podcasts. https://podcasts.apple.com/us/podcast/the-verywell-mind-podcast-with-amy-morin/id1529983509

Morris, Ti. (2018, March 22). *Your clutter archetype and what it says about you*. TISHA MORRIS. https://tishamorris.com/journal/2018/3/22/your-clutter-archetype-and-what-it-says-about-you

Muller, R. T. (2013). *Hoarding as a reaction to trauma*. Psychology Today. https://www.psychologytoday.com/us/blog/talking-about-trauma/201306/hoarding-reaction-trauma

Nest, A. B. (2016, March 30). *10 simple tips to declutter your home*. A Blissful Nest. https://ablissfulnest.com/10-steps-to-declutter-your-home/

Noble, J. (2018, November 11). *Six ways to manage your runaway mind*. Therapy-Den. https://www.therapyden.com/blog/five-ways-to-manage-your-runaway-mind

OrgaNatic. (2019, October 7). *10 genius ideas of MARIE KONDO for ideal home | OrgaNatic*. Www.youtube.com. https://youtu.be/j4D7U3fvlrg

Piedmont. (2019). *Why routines are good for your health*. Piedmont.org. https://www.piedmont.org/living-better/why-routines-are-good-for-your-health

Pinterest, & Hagler, T. (n.d.). *Tracy Hagler writes [Online Image]*. In Pinterest. https://www.pinterest.com/pin/458522805815955080/

Poplin, J. (2018, August 29). *Do this before you start decluttering*. https://www.thesimplicityhabit.com/do-this-before-you-start-decluttering/

Poplin, J. (2019, December 17). *Statistics on clutter that will blow your mind*. The Simplicity Habit. https://www.thesimplicityhabit.com/statistics-on-clutter-that-will-blow-your-mind/

Poplin, J. (2022, May 6). *How much stuff is in the average American home?* The Simplicity Habit. https://www.thesimplicityhabit.com/how-much-stuff-is-in-the-average-american-home/

Post, S. to T. D. (2008, January 23). *The psychology of clutter*. The Denver Post. https://www.denverpost.com/2008/01/23/the-psychology-of-clutter/

Productivity Guy. (2020, July 10). *What is outsourcing | Explained in 2 min*. Www.youtube.com. https://youtu.be/xUD5XJflv-s?t=70

PsychAlive. (2009, June 18). *The critical inner voice explained*. PsychAlive. https://www.psychalive.org/critical-inner-voice/

Psychology Today. (2019). *Positive psychology | Psychology today*. Psychology Today. https://www.psychologytoday.com/us/basics/positive-psychology

Purrington, Mr. (2020, March 25). *Carl Jung on "chaos" – anthology*. Carl Jung Depth Psychology. https://carljungdepthpsychologysite.blog/2020/03/25/carl-jung-on-chaos-anthology/#.YrCuGS8Rqu5 *r/hoarding - Reframing the stigma around uncontrolled clutter: A strength-based approach — MAPP magazine*. (2021). Reddit. https://www.reddit.com/r/hoarding/comments/po90dh/reframing_the_stigma_around_uncontrolled_clutter/

readingraphics. (2019, June 13). *Book summary - The power of now: A guide to spiritual enlightenment*. Readingraphics. https://readingraphics.com/book-summary-the-power-of-now/

Riopel, L. (2019a, September 25). *30 meditation exercises and activities to practice today*. PositivePsychology.com. https://positivepsychology.com/meditation-exercises-activities/

Riopel, L. (2019b, November 28). *28 best meditation techniques for beginners to learn*. PositivePsychology.com. https://positivepsychology.com/meditation-techniques-beginners/

Robbins, T. (n.d.). *How to stop being controlling, 4 effective strategies | Tony Robbins*. Tonyrobbins.com. https://www.tonyrobbins.com/personal-growth/how-to-stop-being-controlling/

Robinson, L. (2019, March 21). *Emotional and psychological trauma*. HelpGuide.org. https://www.helpguide.org/articles/ptsd-trauma/coping-with-emotional-and-psychological-trauma.htm

Sander, L. (2019). *What does clutter do to your brain and body?* NewsGP. https://www1.racgp.org.au/newsgp/clinical/what-does-clutter-do-to-your-brain-and-body

Sanfilippo, M. (2020, March 3). *How to improve your work-life balance*. Business News Daily. https://www.businessnewsdaily.com/5244-improve-work-life-balance-today.html

Schueler, G. (n.d.). *Chaos theory: Interface with Jungian psychology*. In Fisika & Psichica. http://www.psicopolis.com/fisikepsic/orderchaos.htm

Schwartz, S., & Pinterest. (n.d.). *Thich Nhat Hanh Quotes on Instagram: "Breathing in, I know I am breathing i… | Breath in breath out, Thich nhat hanh quotes, Yoga inspiration quotes*. Pinterest. https://www.pinterest.com/pin/505529126924052402/

Shechet, E. (2019, April 2). *How to do nothing: the new guide to refocusing on the real world*. The Guardian. https://www.theguardian.com/lifeandstyle/2019/apr/02/jenny-odell-how-to-do-nothing-attention

Simons, I. (2009). *Why do we have emotions?* Psychology Today. https://www.psychologytoday.com/us/blog/the-literary-mind/200911/why-do-we-have-emotions

Simple Lionheart Life. (2019, July 14). *The negative effects of clutter: 12 ways your stuff is stealing from you!* Simple Lionheart Life. https://simplelionheartlife.com/negative-effects-of-clutter/

Sineriz, M. (2019, January 9). *4 types of clutter: How many are you hanging onto?* Real Estate News & Insights | Realtor.com®. https://www.realtor.com/advice/home-improvement/types-of-clutter-how-to-declutter/

Spellman, L. (2021, February 12). *Episode 124 – guest Caroline Rogers explains positive psychology > The Declutter Hub*. The Declutter Hub. https://declutterhub.com/positive-psychology/

Spittlehouse, J. K. (2016). *Personality associations with mood, hoarding, health and well-being* (pp. iii, 143–162) [PhD Thesis]. https://ourarchive.otago.ac.nz/bitstream/handle/10523/7186/SpittlehouseJanetK2016PhD.pdf?sequence=1&isAllowed=y

Spring Arbor University. (2022). *Fundamentals of communication: 8 basic concepts & definitions | SAU*. Online.arbor.edu. https://online.arbor.edu/news/fundamentals-communication-eight-basic-concepts-and-definitions

*The stigma behind the clutter: 7 myths about hoarding*. (2016, April 14). GoodTherapy.org Therapy Blog. https://www.goodtherapy.org/blog/the-stigma-behind-the-clutter-7-myths-about-hoarding-0414167

StorageCafe. (2022). *Self storage industry trends | StorageCafe*. Www.storagecafe.-com. https://www.storagecafe.com/self-storage-industry-statistics/

Storey, H. (2020, January 6). *Attachment styles and reactions to grief and loss*. Psychology Today. https://www.psychologytoday.com/us/blog/the-freedom-change/202001/attachment-styles-and-reactions-grief-and-loss

Stoycheva, V. (2020, September 26). *The dark side of nostalgia*. Psychology Today. https://www.psychologytoday.com/us/blog/the-everyday-unconscious/202009/the-dark-side-nostalgia

Talks, T. (2017, April 19). *From clutter to clarity | Kerry Thomas | TEDxAshburn*. Www.youtube.com. https://youtu.be/CrsdoIOGCRw

Talks, T. (2018, March 19). *Listen to the monster in your closet | Star Hansen | TEDx-Tucson*. Www.youtube.com. https://youtu.be/qjzvH2wrpDg

TEDxClapham. (2015, February 19). *Judgment. Don't let it frighten you | Aimee Bateman | TEDxClapham*. Www.youtube.com. https://youtu.be/wBTEJsDP-nU

Therapist Aid. (2012). *My fears (worksheet)*. Therapist Aid. https://www.therapis taid.com/therapy-worksheet/my-fears

TherapistAid.com. (2016). *What are personal boundaries?* https://www.therapis taid.com/worksheets/boundaries-psychoeducation-printout.pdf

Theresa. (2022, May 12). *15 connections between clutter and mental health - Practigal Blog*. Practigal Blog. https://www.practigalblog.com/clutter-and-mental-health-connected/

Wang, E. (2022, June 22). *How fast fashion became faster -- and worse for the earth -- The New York Times*. The New York Times.

Ward, M. (2010, October 29). *Facing the fear of not enough*. Possibility Change. https://possibilitychange.com/facing-the-fear-of-not-enough/

Wikipedia Contributors. (2019a, August 3). *21 lessons for the 21st century*. Wikipedia; Wikimedia Foundation. https://en.wikipedia.org/wiki/21_Lessons_for_the_21st_Century

Wikipedia Contributors. (2019b, November 10). *Eyewitness memory*. Wikipedia; Wikimedia Foundation. https://en.wikipedia.org/wiki/Eyewitness_memory

Winters, R. M. (2016). *The hoarding impulse -- suffocation of the soul*. Routledge.

Zen, M. (2021, April 2). *Extreme declutter results ( 95% is GONE!) | Before & after» HOARDER TO MINIMALISM family of 4*. Www.youtube.com. https://youtu.be/VeLg5rDNs-8

Zen, M. (2022, June 12). *10 minimalist habits that will transform your life!* Www.youtube.com. https://youtu.be/rUnpOplJulM

# ABOUT THE AUTHOR

Renata Roberts is a qualified Master life coach with degrees in Psychology and Applied Theology and the author of "What if I don't have enough? A guide to understanding mental and physical clutter. She is a life coach, motivational speaker, and trainer. Her career has been spent studying the influence of trauma, social pressure, and emotional challenges on our ability to reach our full potential and live extraordinary lives.

Renata advocates for the principles of intentional living and is passionate about helping people engage with their own life and prioritizing their mental and physical health.

Her strong values and faith are the main influences in her approach to life. She shares her home with her husband, children, and pets. She knows how chaotic life can be and uses humor, a positive perspective, and not taking herself too seriously as weapons against mental and physical clutter in her own life.

Made in the USA
Las Vegas, NV
20 September 2024